THIS IS ME
NO DARKNESS TOO DEEP

May this book bless
you copies are available
bo buy from

www.fionamylesauthor.com.

FIONA MYLES

This Is Me
No Darkness Too Deep

Authored by Fiona Myles
© Fiona Myles 2021
Cover Design: Marcia M Publishing House
Cover Photography: Fiona Myles
Edited by Marcia M Publishing House Editorial Team, Lee Dickinson
Published by Marcia M Spence of Marcia M Publishing House,
West Bromwich, West Midlands the UNITED KINGDOM B71 1JB on behalf of
Fiona Myles
All rights reserved 2021 Marcia M Publishing House

www.marciampublishing.com

DEDICATION

I would like to dedicate the book to my dear friends who are no longer with us.

John McQuarrie - You taught me everything on generosity and grace.

Barry Hill - You told me everything about everybody and made me laugh like no one else has since you died.

Kerrie Killeen - Your beautiful Spirit was a joy to work with in the Women's Home, the funniest girl with the biggest smile.

Zedenka Yabani - You never failed to call me just at the right time always reassuring me that my child was coming.

Each one of you are so fondly remembered by many - Each one of you so unique in your walk with God I learned so much from each of your lives.

Acknowledgements

This has been such a long journey to get from Blank to book. I'm grateful to God for giving me the strength to keep writing to get my story out there.

I want to thank my Husband Brian Myles for his unending patience with me especially in the run-up to publication.

I thank Tarnya Coley for her epic nudge gifting Plan it See it Anticipate it

My thanks go to my church Victory Outreach for just being there for me too many people to mention but you do all know who you are.

To my Pastors, Paul and Vicky Lloyd of Victory Outreach Manchester - your love and patience with me over nearly 20 years have been incredible. Thank you

My family is important to me I acknowledge all of my family members, parents, siblings, cousins, aunties and uncles you are all important to me.

Thank you

FOREWORD

Fiona is a dear friend and co labourer in Christ, I have known Fiona for over 20 years witnessing her journey and growth in Christ and as a woman. I have watched her transformation in action, the many ups and downs that she speaks of in this book and watched as she negotiated them. My husband Paul and I had the privilege of being at their wedding. She has served faithfully in the church for many years in diverse roles. She has worked in our administrative team, she managed our women's recovery home for four years seeing many lives transformed. Her heart for broken women is a beautiful thing and she diligently walks alongside people for years and I commend her for that. Her faith and Trust in the Lord saw her receive the promise of a child, like sarah in the bible when it looked utterly impossible God blessed her and her husband with a child.

Not only is she a wife and Mother she is also a leader, a responsible hard worker who is diligent in all that she does. This book is a roller coaster of emotions and victory a hard to put down read for anyone looking for a story of hope.

I believe this is Fionas time to shine and I pray for her life to be like the Apostle Paul, a drink offering being poured out to touch others.

Vicky Lloyd
Senior Pastors Wife
Victory Outreach Manchester

THIS IS ME
NO DARKNESS TOO DEEP

It was the 27th of December 1988, and I had been drinking solid for two days. Christmas had come and gone in a blur; so much had gone wrong in such a short space of time. How had my life plummeted to this?

I had been married to Simon for only two years – but it had been a traumatic two years. He was a drinker, and was prone to taking out his every frustration on me. I had the scars to prove it. Simon and I had parted ways permanently now that he was with my half-sister; the one that I had just discovered after finding my natural mother (I had been adopted as a small baby). I had run away from the whole sorry situation, back to Glasgow from London. My aunt had a flat 21 storeys up in the heart of the Gorbals, next door to her son. She just claimed her giro from it and didn't live there, because she lived with my uncle in Ibrox. It was a bit sparse, but it was somewhere to lay my head and try to make sense of the past five years of my life. I couldn't get any peace in my mind: everything was rolled up into one big ball of pain, hurt and of complete rejection. I felt totally finished – finished, at 22? I felt I had nothing to live for, that I had let everyone down again, let myself down again. I could see no hope – what was going to become of me? I seemed to have no control over any part of my life. Thoughts were spinning round so quickly. Nobody really wanted me; I wasn't truly loved by anyone. It's easy to say it, but I had never really felt it.

I decided there and then it was time to end my misery. Tiger Tim had just finished his nightly programme on the radio and was singing his wee tune, "What are you going to do after the Tiger's gone?" I knew right away I was going to end my life by jumping off the balcony of the flats I was in. I slid off the couch I was lying on, and made my way to the balcony. It was a nice balcony with a chair in it and a couple of sorry-looking plants.

The walk to the door of the balcony seemed endless. I managed to unlock the door and step out onto the balcony. The lights all around the city were blinking and flickering and all I could think about were the happy families and people in those houses, feeling loved and being loved by others.

I stepped closer to the edge of the balcony and leaned my head on the wall; the sadness inside me was overwhelmingly massive. I felt sad about what I was intending to do, sad that my mum and dad would be upset, but I also fully believed they would be relieved in a strange kind of way. I knew that there was no other way. It had to end: I could not as a human being endure any more pain, fear, rejection or abuse.

I managed to get myself sitting on the edge of the wall with my legs dangling over the balcony, which was no mean feat. I was terrified – even in the fog of alcohol I was scared of what I was about to do, but I could see no other way to get past this episode of my life, even knowing I was the person to blame for most of it.

I took a deep breath and pushed myself off. I hit the ground very quickly and realised I was still alive. It was an incredible feeling of fear and anger mixed together. I thought that I must be very badly injured, and could not believe I had survived a drop from 21 storeys. I wondered if I was actually dead and that was what it felt like. Could I sit up and look around me? Yes, I could because, unbelievably, I had landed backwards into the balcony! To this day, I do not know how I managed to push myself backwards into the balcony. Or was it divine intervention?

I feel that I should explain how I got to that low point in my life.

I was born in March 1966. I was a normal healthy baby with an amazing shock of jet-black hair. I was born in Dumfries, Scotland, to Margaret Kirkpatrick. Margaret had another daughter called Dorothy, who was already three years old. Me (Helen) and Dorothy were both illegitimate, which in those days in such a small town was really a shameful thing. Our father was a man named Roy Nesbitt, who managed the hotel Margaret was employed in. Roy was married, so could do nothing to support Margaret and his two children.

Margaret's mother, Jessie, had agreed to look after Dorothy when she was born so that Margaret could support herself and her daughter. When I was born, Jessie was so upset that it had happened again, but agreed to look after me as well. Jessie's husband was called Hugh, and he worked for the Forestry Commission. They lived in a tiny village called Glentrool. What a beautiful place it is, and well worth a visit.

A tragedy occurred in June, three months after my birth, when my grandad, Hugh, died of a heart attack. The family were devastated and found it very hard to cope. Jessie, sadly, had to tell Margaret she could not look after two children on her own. Dorothy was older and running about, so it was decided that Sally, who was

Margaret's younger sister, would take care of me. Sally had two boys, so was ecstatic to have a little girl to make a fuss over. Lawrence was the same age as Dorothy and Ian was the same age as me. Sally was just getting used to having me around when she discovered that she was pregnant again. Shortly after that, Margaret agreed to put me into care and up for adoption. Sally was devastated. She tried to assure Margaret she would cope with all of us, no problem, but Margaret knew I had to go into care. So off I went with my little bag of things into social care.

After a while, along came Patsy and Bobby Cochrane, who were looking to adopt a child as a sister or brother to their only child, Gavin. One look at my cheeky wee fat face and shock of black hair was all it took. Before long, my mum and dad were settling me into their home in Dumfries. I was a very happy baby. Mum and Dad decided to call me Fiona, and kept my original name, Helen, as my middle name. My big brother Gavin accepted me, no problem. Two years later, along came a little sister for Gavin and me. Mhairi was a beautiful little curly-haired girl. We lived in Dumfries as a family until I was four.

My father's job caused us to move to Perth in 1970. I remember Margaret sadly telling me that she used to look for a little girl with long black hair and a limp in Dumfries. I had been born with a congenital hip and was in a splint for a while as a baby. She had presumed we had stayed in the area and believed I would have had a limp. I always feel sad when I think of those times she may have thought she had seen me, not knowing I was miles and miles away.

When I was five years old, we moved to a very small village called Glenochil, which I loved. I had two sets of lovely grandparents, but I really felt at home with Nana and Grandpa, who were Dad's parents. I loved it when Dad would say we were going to Nana's. I saw a lot of them because they didn't live very far away, whereas Granny and Grandad lived hundreds of miles away. I really loved them too, but I hated the long drive to their house because it made me car sick.

We had great fun with Grandad. He was a real storyteller, and used to tell us tales of bears and lions that lived in the woods behind their house, and he would take us out to follow their tracks very carefully. I really believed him until I realised he was making it all up, and also making the tracks to keep us going. He was fantastic at stories. My granny was a great cook and she knitted and crocheted us matching jumpers and waistcoats – real 70s bobby-dazzlers, and people would love them nowadays when vintage is all the rage. I used to marvel at the way Granny would set the table with a little dish of this and a little dish of that, and bread on a plate and beautiful silver dishes with butter curls that she made herself with a silver butter curler. Then the dinner would come in big dishes to help ourselves from. I still think about how she made such a lovely big job of the dinner. I wondered, though, if she did it all the time or was it just special because we didn't really go very often because they lived so far away, up north. I suspect Granny did it all the time, because she did bed and breakfast for people over the years.

Nana and Grandad, who lived fairly close to us, were less formal. She would give us our dinner on the little table in the living room after we played Ludo and watched the wrestling. One thing I remember at Nana's that I didn't really like was getting up really early to have porridge and scrape out the fire! Don't get me wrong here, I loved the open fire, but it was a rotten job getting it ready for the day's fire.

Nana had a funny, white, little poodle called Puffles and, to this day, I swear I will have a poodle and it will be called Puffles What a name to give a dog. We really didn't like having to take it out for a walk; if she ran off, the last thing you wanted to shout out in public as a child was Puffles! Puffles did not live up to her cute name; she was a maniac! She would bare her teeth at you for nothing and bite you just for good luck; Puffles was a bad-tempered poodle! It's only now as a grown-up that I realise poor wee Puffles was probably very sweet, but we tormented the poor dog. I'm sure when she heard Dad's car pull up outside, she would groan inside and pray we didn't stay long.

Anyway, you know when people say to you what's the first real memory you have? I seem to have three of them, all rolled into one, and whenever I try to separate them to try and work out which one was first, I get really mixed up. So I will tell it as I see it in my head. First of all, I'm running down an embankment in Perth after my brother and a couple of other boys. I think I was getting to be the annoying little sister by this point. We all get into this field and start playing hide and seek, but because it was boys, you had to shoot the person you found! Then it switches to me on a little blue bike with white tyres, and Dad is holding the back of it trying to encourage me to just pedal and go. I can remember pedalling with great confidence until I realised that Dad had let go, when I promptly fell off! Then it switches to me and my brother getting out of a car and him shutting my finger in the door. Dad was great at first aid, and would whip out the iodine and plasters in a flash when we came in bleeding and cut. When I spoke to Dad about this cinematic first memory, he reckons it all happened in the one day, with the fingers in the door first, then the bike, then the playing with my brother and his friends. He thinks it was the trauma of the finger thing that made me retain the whole day's events in my memory.

The next set of memories after that are from Glenochil Village, where we moved next when I was five. I have the greatest of memories from the years I lived in the village. Mum and Dad always told me I was very special and had been chosen, and all the things you're supposed to encourage an adopted child with. It fell on deaf ears; I didn't understand all that was being said. I would say I didn't really get a handle on the 'being adopted' thing until I was about eight or nine. Mum told me the social workers had advised her to tell me from an early age that I was chosen, special, wanted and all those kinds of adjectives, as it would be easier for me to digest the news that I was not really their own child, but somebody else's. I don't really think that any worker of any level of education can guess what that information can do to a little mind.

I know that my mind found it all a bit too much to handle, and I started to go off the rails. I was getting into trouble at school and in the village, doing really crazy things there was no way I would get away with, as it was such a small place. There were only about 70 houses in our village, and everybody knew me. One episode that really sticks out was a time I took my sister's favourite teddy bear and gave it a name. I then went around all the doors in the village raffling off guesses at the bear's name for five pence. A girl called Marianne won it, and I remember was very reluctant to give it back! Unfortunately, my older brother was punished more than me, as he had to escort me around the village explaining what I had done and paying everyone back the money they had given.

I remember breaking into someone's house and stealing KitKats, then sitting on top of garages in full view of everyone, eating them. By the time I was 10, things were getting tense; I was feeling different, like I had something mad going on inside. I was always thinking up stuff and telling the most outrageous stories; they were not even clever, because they were so easily found out. I stole my brother's paper money that he had worked hard for. I started to be a pain at school. I would do really bad things. I slammed a door on a guy's hand, deliberately, to hurt him.

I had a moment where I nearly killed a two or three-year-old boy. I was about 10, and had taken him out to the park for his mum because she was really ill. I was playing with him for a while, got bored and started to annoy him to make him whine. I got fed up with the whining and stuck his head in a puddle to keep him quiet. He could have drowned if someone hadn't come along. I still wonder to this day if he has any memory of that happening.

I was getting regular punishments for my bad behaviour. If I had been fighting, I would be kept in, and if I had done worse, I would be smacked. I remember getting the belt off Dad for swearing at a teacher and, to this day, I still get mad about that, because I didn't swear at her: she misheard what I said. But because I would lie and deny every accusation put my way and be found to be lying, this time there was no mercy.

Now that I am older, I think to myself that I didn't really need to be punished. I was struggling to understand what was being said to me. I was different, looked different, and behaved differently. I was a swirling mass of mental incapacity. I know there were times when Mum and Dad talked about sending me to a List D school, as I think they were called. It was a type of approved school where troubled children were sent if their parents couldn't manage their behaviour. I don't know why they didn't, but I am glad they chose to keep me. I'm thankful I had great parents who endured so much from me and my madness, but continued to care for me and did their best to set me straight.

At the age of 12, the most traumatic event of my life took place. You may be waiting to read about a death, a huge trauma or something, but for me this was massive. We moved house from Glenochil to Tullibody near the town of Alloa. I hated it. I hated the house. I hated my room and, most of all, I hated my parents for taking me away to this horrible place and away from my real Mum. Suddenly, I was blaming them at this time for stealing me away. My brain went into some kind of meltdown. I began to dislike everyone and everything. I felt abandoned, rejected, unwanted. Everything crumbled in my life and in my mind. We are now embarking on the very messed-up journey of someone whose hormones have leapt into life and they can't handle it!

I took a real dislike to my younger sister as it seemed to me that, for my parents, she could do no wrong. I'm sure she did do wrong, but I was getting to a real crisis in my young life. I was confused and upset about being told I wasn't really their child. I think I had difficulty expressing how I felt and it came out in bizarre behaviour. As I launched into my teens, all hell broke loose. I started swearing, drinking and smoking, and my parents could do nothing right! They were the bad ones, not me!

One night, when they had gone out, I decided to cut myself quite badly and lie out in the drive so they would think something bad had happened to me. That didn't work out as planned, and I just ended up with a very sore leg.

My next move was an attempt to kill my little sister during the night by trying to suffocate her with a carrier bag. I was crying out for help, but in totally the wrong way. I also got caught creeping round the house with a huge knife in the middle of the night. My mind was an absolute labyrinth of craziness.

Mum and Dad had no clue what to do with me, and I couldn't explain what was going on inside, so off I went to a psychiatrist. The sessions resolved nothing. I actually have no memory of them at all. My mother did tell me that it didn't last long, as I wouldn't speak to him. I didn't find out until I was 18 that Mum crushed diazepam that the psychiatrist prescribed into my dinner so I would sleep, because a lot of the scary stuff was happening during the night. My head was still a mess. I continually felt bad, sad and scared. I really didn't know who I was or what I was doing.

At one point, during my secondary school days, I went for the weekend to stay with one of my classmates. She had an older brother who introduced us to pornographic magazines. I was amazed by them and they had me enthralled. He took me through to his room one night and performed a sex act on me that I didn't really understand, but couldn't get out of my mind. I stopped going to that friend's house not long after because the things that were happening there were beginning to get a little scary. Did I tell anyone what had happened? No, of course not. Would I have been believed? I don't know.

I got through school with not one O level or anything. Due to my bad behaviour, I was not attending classes and not co-operating in other classes. I spent quite a lot of time in detention and the headmaster's office. I was always the instigator in trouble, not the follower. At high school, my teachers would always ask why could I not be like my older brother, and when my little sister came up, teachers would say to her they hoped she was not like her sister. Always different.

As soon as I left school, Mum and Dad helped me to get a live-in job quite far away from where we lived. I wasn't afraid of change and thought I would love being away from home. I hated it, and got the sack very quickly for cheek and stealing.

I got another job where the lady knew I was trouble but had decided to give me a chance. I was there for a couple of weeks trying to fit in. One night in the bar, one of the ghillies who took people out fishing on the lochs was helping me to choose whether I liked vodka with orange in it or with blackcurrant? I was 16. I had been in a couple of serious clinches with guys, but had never had sex. Even though things had happened to me at my friend's house, it wasn't full sex. Completely drunk, I remember him taking me to an empty room in the hotel and forcing himself on me. I remember being really scared but too numb to do anything about it because the drink had the better of me. When he was finished, he pushed me out of the window into the nettles and bushes below. I woke up the next day in agony and bleeding heavily. I couldn't go to work and stayed in bed all day pretending I had the flu. I challenged him about what he did to me, and he just laughed and called me names, saying it was all my own doing.

I ran away from there after a few months with a girl called Jean to a place in Forfar. We didn't last too long in an abandoned house with no money and no heating. It wasn't exactly a great idea and ended fairly swiftly. We were both just 16. I ended up having to ask my parents to pay my fare home from Dundee.

I wasn't home long before I was off again, this time to be a nanny in London. Mum and Dad thought I was good with kids. They didn't know about the neighbour's kid I'd tried to drown in a puddle. I suppose I did like children, but I wasn't really nanny material, as it turned out.

So, at 17 years of age, off I went to Hendon with my little burgundy suitcase and my new blue coat with white fur inside, and a lovely blue and white Fair Isle beret and scarf my granny had given me the previous Christmas. *A new start; let's see if I can get this right.*

Off I went to a family with two boys: David and Edward. I was only six years older than David, and it turned out I was not the nanny, but really just the general dogsbody with looking after the children thrown in. I did all the cooking, all the cleaning and picked the boys up from school. I was lucky that Mum and Dad had taught me well about cleaning, ironing and cooking, so it wasn't a shock to my system, but I got bored really quickly. The drudgery of the same thing day in and day out at 17 was too much for me. I had joined this nannies' union thing in Hendon, which was a glorified drinking excuse for a crowd of bored young girls that were being exploited in people's homes. Someone should make a film about this. I soon left my job. I just packed my bag and disappeared on them. Imagine doing that these days?

I got another job in Mill Hill with a couple who had one little boy and a dry cleaning business. I was the one who ironed the shirts all day. Honestly, it was a job description malfunction again, because I was the general dogsbody, making someone else a fortune.

I left that job when everyone was out again, but this time I took a few pieces of jewellery with me. I was a bit stuck this time: my mum and dad were getting fed up with me leaving jobs and them having to bail me out. Before going off to London, I had about three other jobs in hotels or people's houses that I messed up. I got a job cleaning in a bar. They had a jukebox and I always played Queen's *I Want to Break Free* as I strutted my stuff up and down the bar with the vacuum cleaner.

The last job I had as a nanny, I remember going to work for a family in Borehamwood. They were very wealthy but paying me pennies to do all their work in the house, so I decided to sign on. Some of the other nannies were doing it, so I thought I would too. I wasn't really clued up about the social and all that. As soon as the family found out, they sacked me on the spot! Off I went with my little burgundy suitcase and my blue coat. I had lost track of the Fair Isle beret and scarf. I had nowhere to go and it was night-time. They had given me what they thought they owed me as wages, but that was only £20. I slept that night in a train station photo booth. Don't ask me how I slept, but I did. I phoned the nanny agency the next day to see if they could help me, but they had taken me off their books; I had earned myself quite a bad name as a nanny!

I headed into the city and decided to try to get another job. I didn't really know where to look and I didn't really know where to go. I wasn't going to tell my parents what was happening, so I was 17 years old and alone in London. I just phoned them now and again. After a few nights in Victoria Station, I signed on and had a list of homeless hostels to check out. I decided I would be happier in the station. I lived in and around Victoria Railway Station for around two months. I enjoyed going round and round the underground getting on and not really getting off until the end of the day. You would be amazed at what people forget to take off the train with them.

I realised I needed to get somewhere to stay, so I found a hotel in Finsbury Park that took people on the DHSS. It was the Queens Hotel run by some Greek Cypriot family. I spent my time wandering about and going in and out of the city. I would sit in the bar of the hotel at night chatting to folks. I met some incredible characters in there.

The manager of the hotel approached me one night and asked if I would like to have a drink with him and his friend, a young girl called Danielle. Danielle was 19, just a couple of years older than me. She was nice and friendly and, over the next three weeks, I spent all my time with her and the manager. They took me out, bought me clothes and drinks and food. I was loving it and was feeling very loved and special.

Danielle asked me if I wanted to move in with her at her flat in Finsbury Park. I thought she was brilliant and said I would love to. I moved in and when she took me to my room, the wardrobe was full of clothes that she said were mine to wear. I thought it was a bit dodgy, but went along with it, as my option was to go back to the station or the hotel. Danielle took me out that night and, after a few drinks, started to explain the situation – that now and again we would have to 'entertain' some of the manager's friends in payment for having the flat and clothes and everything. At first I was shocked, and thought I couldn't do it, but Danielle was very persuasive and told me it wasn't that bad for what we were getting. Two days later, she came in and told me to get ready for the night as "friends" were coming. I was a bit scared as I didn't really know how it was going to be. When 8 p.m. came, the door was knocked on, and my heart was in my mouth as I opened it to three much older, foreign-looking men. In they came and we had drinks and food, and then it was time to entertain them. It wasn't too bad, but it wasn't too nice either! When they had gone, Danielle was so nice to me, telling me how well I had done, and I started to feel quite all right about it.

This went on two or three times a week for a couple of months. One night the entertainment was filmed. I was always full of alcohol, so nothing was really that bad. The men always left the money with Danielle, which she put in the kitchen drawer. The manager of the hotel I had stayed in would come and take it the next day after the visitors had been. It got boring and I knew I didn't want to keep doing it, so I decided I had had enough of that lifestyle and wanted to move on. How? How could I get out of it? We had 'entertained' four times that week, and I was getting the impression it was going to get busier! I went to the drawer one morning, took all the money that was in it and walked out the door with what I could put in an orange rucksack. *What do I do now?*

I had to get as far away as possible from Finsbury Park. I thought I would try to get another live-in nanny job. I got some magazines I knew advertised live-in positions, called a couple of numbers and managed to get myself a live-in position in Finchley. It was more of an au pair position, and I had quite a lot of free time. I went to the local pubs and met a crowd of Irish men I got on with really well. They were funny and nice to me. After a while, I met a man called Mick, who was much older than me but so very charming and funny. He asked me to move in with him after only a couple of weeks. I moved into his house. I was just coming to the end of being 17. He lived a weird existence: a perfectly ordinary electrician by day, and a sex maniac at night! We got involved in swinging sessions and lots of pornography and stuff like that. I just did it, as it seemed to me that all these people were perfectly normal during the day, and just had an extraordinary way of enjoying themselves at night. After what I had endured previously, it was actually really good fun.

Mick was a heavy drinker and had a bit of a temper. One night after a really heavy session, he was pestering me and I was not interested, so he started laying into me. He threw me out of the bed and started kicking me. The last thing that I remember is being thrown against the bedroom wall. I woke up the next day in hospital; I was hurting everywhere. A nurse was there when I woke up. She was patting my hand and asking me if I was OK? I tried to sit up but couldn't manage it. I asked her what was wrong with me and how long I would be in the hospital. She told me that she was really sorry to tell me, but I had lost my baby. I was shocked: I didn't have a baby. I started to cry because I was confused and in pain. Later, the nurse explained I had been 20 weeks' pregnant and had lost a little boy. I called him Thomas.

Some of the neighbours came to see me in the hospital, which was nice of them. Most of them were friends of Mick, so I was surprised to see them. They wanted to know what had happened and were shocked about the whole thing. I think it was the baby being lost that upset them the most, even though none of us knew I was pregnant.

Mick never came to see me. When it was time for me to leave, I realised I had nowhere to go. I knew enough not to go back to live with him! One of the neighbours came and got me and let me stay for a few nights until I got sorted out. I found a hostel in Highbury that was willing to take me in. The night before I left, one of the neighbours came to the door and said we had to go outside. Outside were a group of men with Mick in the middle. He was crying and pleading with the guys. One of the men motioned me to come forward and asked me how many weeks pregnant had I been? As soon as I said 20, they started to beat him. I tried to run away, but they forced me to watch. It was one of the most frightening moments in my life; it made me sick to think they were doing it for what he had done to me.

So on I went in my journey, still feeling even more unwanted and disliked than before, and a new feeling was emerging of shame at what I had been doing sexually.

The next day me and my orange rucksack left for Highbury. The blue coat was now a distant memory too. What a dump that place was. I was sharing a tiny room with a girl called Debbie. I soon realised Debbie was a 'working girl'. She very quickly introduced me to smoking hash and dropping acid. I took to it like a duck to water. It was great! I could lose myself in a fog of drugs, not having to feel anything. I started to go out with her and started to turn some tricks myself. I loved it, probably because I was off my head by this time. I had been through a lot and the drugs were great for not thinking about any of it. I was making money and having a fantastic time with Debbie. She taught me so much about street life. I was such a country bumpkin to her; I didn't know any of the slang for stuff and I didn't know how to con the social. By the time Debbie was finished with me, I was an expert in a few fields I didn't even know existed! Debbie liked me. *At last, someone actually likes me.*

Eventually it all came to an end one night when I was in my room alone. Someone knocked on the door and, as I answered it, two guys from the hostel pushed their way into the room. They were drunk and started to hit me and call me names like whore, prostitute, etc. They were really on a roll. I knew at that moment that what was about to happen may very well be the last thing that ever happened to me. I realised I was extremely vulnerable; the place that I was staying in was not the kind of place where heroes came running if someone screamed. They began by pushing me around a bit, and I kept saying to them I would do what they wanted, but not to hurt me. I got a punch in the face for that and I fell to the floor. They jumped on me and started to rip off my clothes. They took it in turns to abuse me in more than one way. I was in agony, and blood was pouring from my head and mouth where they had hit me. I never passed out during this attack and can remember every detail as if it was yesterday.

When they finally gave up their assault, they left me lying in the room bleeding. My friend Debbie took me to the hospital for a check over to make sure nothing was broken. The only thing they broke that night was my spirit. After all that I had been through, I was a wreck. I started hanging out with a really bad crew from Liverpool who were known for their drug and drink abuse. I was still only 18 years old and very confused, hurt and broken as a person. I got quite heavily involved with taking acid and speed; I loved the way I could just zone out with the drink on top.

After a while, a few of us moved out of the hostel into a shared house. Debbie came as well. After the attack, I didn't turn tricks any more, but I really liked Debbie, so we stayed together. Debbie was a bit of a risk-taker, and got into quite a few mad situations. We had been hanging around for a couple of months with that lot and I took up with an older guy called Terry. Terry was quite quiet, but he was the ringleader of the group. He was the one that got the drugs for everyone and sold the stuff down the pub. Debbie and I decided one night after a particularly mad session to steal the next lot of acid that came in. For what reason, I do not know; I just kind of got pulled along with the idea and, when the time came, I pulled the strips out of the hem of the curtain and took the money that Terry had stashed, and off we went.

We headed for Scotland, as Debbie had a granny we could stay with. When we got there, we settled in and started to spend some of the money. Debbie said she knew someone that could give us good money for the drugs. Off she went, and I never saw her again. I stayed a few days at Debbie's gran's but knew that she would not be back. I felt totally betrayed and hurt by what she had done. I thought she was my friend but, again, everything inside was shattered. What would I do? Where would I go?

I called Mum and Dad, and went home to lick my wounds. I had concocted some story about just being up for a visit, but knew that I couldn't stay long. Mum and Dad knew nothing of all that had been going on, as I would call them periodically and tell them whatever I thought they would like to hear.

Four days later, as I was preparing to go back to London, Terry came to the door! I will never, never, never forget the fear I felt when I saw him standing in my parents' living room. I didn't know what to do. My parents had no idea of the life I was leading, so how could I tell them this man was probably going to kill me? Mum thought he was charming. He actually was charming, and they thought it was lovely he had come all that way to find me because I had broken his heart! I knew that my mum was not going to hear me if I even attempted to tell her the truth. I was totally and utterly consumed with terror.

So Terry and I went back to London. He only said one thing to me all the way back to London – that he was going to kill me. We went back to the hostel and he asked for a room in the attic area, which was a horrible bit of the hostel. There were really thin little hallways and rooms only on one side of them. I was so scared that I couldn't even cry. I knew that, deep in my heart, I was destined to die. A part of me thought it was probably for the best, considering all that had gone before, so I just resigned myself to it. Terry would go out now and again and lock me in. He dared me to try to leave the room. I wasn't allowed to even go to the toilet or the shower rooms; I had to go to the toilet in the bin and wash in the sink, if allowed. Terry treated me like a dog. He would do things to me that would make me think that was it, that he was going to strangle me or suffocate me. He would let me go at the last minute. A couple of times I passed out and thought that I had died, but unfortunately I hadn't.

Eventually, an opportunity presented itself for escape: a cleaner opened the door and asked to clean the room. I couldn't believe it. I took right off out that door with nothing but what I could carry in my arms. I knocked on some doors to get some help or some money to get me as far away from the hostel as I could.

A guy called Simon, who was from Scotland and remembered me from the last time I had been in the hostel, let me into his room. When I explained as much as I could about the situation I was in, he said he would help me. Terry went mental when he realised that I had gone; he was running around the place kicking doors in and screaming. I hid under the bed for two days.

Simon knew some guys in another part of London that would house us until we could get away. Simon was now my hero; my knight in shining armour. He had friends and family in southern Ireland that he was going to take me to. The difficult part was getting out of the hostel. We decided to creep out of one of the fire exit doors at three o'clock one morning. I ran and ran as fast as I could to get clear of the place. I think Simon thought I was running away from him! In hindsight, maybe I should have kept running.

We arrived at a house in Hornsey about five o'clock. No one was up but Simon had a key. I didn't wake up until that night about ten o'clock. Simon had explained the situation to his mates. They were happy to let us stay until we had the money for the boat to Ireland. They were a rough bunch, but friendly enough. Their place was really dirty, with ants and mice all over the place. After a while I realised they were fanatical about being Irish; they told lots of stories about the troubles from their perspective, which was Catholic. Simon told me to keep quiet about not being a Catholic. I wasn't really anything anyway, but I asked him lots of questions about being a Catholic and passed muster when questioned by the guys. One Saturday night after a lot of drinking and carrying on, one of the guys pulled a gun on another guy, which instantly silenced the whole room. I remember thinking to myself that this was the longest moment of my life. I was petrified because I didn't know what was going to happen, but the rest of the guys jumped him and got the gun from him and dragged the other guy out the door and left him there all night.

I was, more and more, becoming dependent on drugs and drink to keep me from going over the edge. I was always scared of what was going to happen to me, and always panicking that somehow the people who had already done their best to destroy me would somehow find me and kill me. I would be paranoid about getting murdered for many, many years when, really, the possibility of anyone finding me or even really wanting to was truly remote. In my head, though, it was imminent.

Eventually we headed over the sea to southern Ireland. Simon had been living in Ireland before he came to England to support his pregnant girlfriend, but when they got to England she dumped him and had the baby on her own. It was difficult for me when we arrived in Ireland, because all his friends thought he would be bringing back his girlfriend and baby once they had married. Instead there was me: nutcase, messed-up Scot.

I was introduced to everyone and taken to the house we were going to be staying in. Boy, what a shock I got. The house was a dump, filthy, with years of grime and neglect. The kitchen was full of rubble where the ceiling had fallen in, and there were rats' claw prints in the grease that was in the frying pan. I became a bit chameleon-like, able to merge into different situations very quickly, and I adjusted to my new way of life because I was just so grateful to get away from the nutter who wanted to kill me.

We spent our days sleeping and our nights smoking hash and being hippies to the max. I thought I was so happy and so cool singing Woody Guthrie and Bob Dylan songs, not washing except in the lake with a bar of soap and eating what we could steal from the shop or from the fields surrounding us. I couldn't get any dole money because I had to be means tested, which took forever in such a rural area. We used to break up the furniture in the house to make a fire to cook anything that we found that was edible.

I called home every so often and let on that I was OK. In a way I was OK, but Mum would not have thought so if she had been able to see the place where we were living. After a while, the local Gardai (police) started to harass us because we were very unusual. There were three brothers, Simon and I all living in the house at the time. One evening when I was coming back from the pub, I got picked up in the police car and taken to the station. They grilled me for hours about what was going on in the house. They said they were going to get an order to have me thrown out of Ireland because I was living with all these men. Simon and I decided to get married to see if that would help. We went to the local chapel and were told that they didn't do mixed marriages – I had to convert to Catholicism! I was up for that; I didn't really care about becoming a Catholic. As far as I was concerned, I didn't have a religion anyway.

So off we went to take the classes for me to be converted. It was all going very well until, strangely, one day such a fear came over me about what I was doing. I didn't really understand anything about religion, but what I did know was that Dad had a thing about Catholics, the English and foreigners. I didn't follow it through. I knew that if I did it, Dad would be really hurt and angry. It was going to be bad enough bringing a Catholic home! I really didn't know how Mum and Dad were going to take the news that I was going to be getting married to a complete stranger, as far as they were concerned. And a Catholic to boot!

We had to move to another house down the road, far enough away from the old house but near enough to the contacts we had for the speed and hash we were getting through. It really wasn't easy to get drugs in southern Ireland's beautiful countryside in the early eighties. We decided to get a dog for our house and try to be normal. The dog took ill with poison from one of the fields around us and we had to strangle it to stop it suffering.

It was around this time that I had my first seizure. It was quite scary for Simon because I apparently went into some kind of coma and woke up in the hospital. Once I told them my lifestyle, they were quick to put it down to that and sent me home. I was still only 18 years old.

We started to get real hassle from the locals, because it was no secret that we were not married, and that was just not on in their area! The fact that we were on drugs, and lots of them, didn't really help us to blend into the community! We knew our days in Ireland were numbered, and we had to think about what we were we going to do? After a couple of days of weighing up the options, of which there were few, we decided to move to Glasgow. Glasgow! I was a bit worried about this, because I had heard many a story about the hard Glaswegians! But Simon had family there and assured me that, really, this was the best thing for us. We were still intending to get married, so that spurred me on towards the move, as I had some kind of fairy tale imaginings about what marriage would be like. My only templates for marriage were Mum and Dad and grandparents, who were all very happily married. My thoughts were that all this madness would subside and marriage would make me normal, like Mum and Dad.

We took a rucksack each, filled it with whatever we could get in it, and just walked out of the house, leaving it in a real state, and hitchhiked all the way to Larne from County Cavan in southern Ireland. We got as far as Armagh on the first day and decided to camp near the border in a field. We put up our little tent, found a shop, bought some booze and settled down for the night intending to hitch the rest of the way the next day. The next morning, we woke up to shouts of, "Come out of there with your hands up!"

Simon crawled out first. I thought I was going to faint. When I came out they had Simon with a gun in his face, and they did the same to me as they ransacked our meagre belongings. I was aware of the troubles, but didn't think I would ever get caught up in them. We were told to lie down on our faces, and once they had looked through everything we had, I think they realised we were two stupid drunks and just walked away telling us to get the **** out of there as fast as we could. I can tell you it took less than 10 minutes for us to pack up and get the **** out of there. I think my legs shook all the way to Larne!

We made it to Larne and had enough to get the boat to Stranraer in Scotland. Home at last, back in Scotland. We pitched up our tent on the beach that night, thinking it was so romantic. We were rudely awakened by high winds blowing the tent away into the sea that had crept up the beach during the night. When I think about that night, to this day it makes me laugh! Once we had gathered up what we had left, we headed to the nearest road going in the Glasgow direction. We didn't get offered a lift until nearly 11 a.m. A coach stopped, and he was going all the way to Glasgow. Yippee!

We arrived at Simon's mum and dad's house that night, absolutely stinking and starving. We got fed and had a wash and change of clothes. I called Mum and let her know I was in the vicinity and not to worry, because I was staying with friends in Glasgow. We went straight to the social and signed up for crisis payments and homeless money and anything else we could get. One of our mates had met us in Glasgow, but he couldn't get any money or benefits because he was Irish.

We were going to visit my mum and dad the next day to introduce them to Simon. We were still intending to get married but not really knowing how to go about it. We went to the local registry office to ask. The first thing was that we had to get an address; we were still registered as homeless as we were just dossing on the floor of Simon's mum's living room.

Our friend decided to go home; he didn't like the fast pace of the city. We moved into a room in an area of Glasgow called Cessnock. The room was really cheap and the social were happy to pay it for us. We found out the reason it was so cheap when we moved in: it was right above Cessnock underground station and the rumbling of the train going round and round was really annoying; it made everything in the room rattle and shake.

At this point, I thought life was getting better, and I was really looking forward to getting married. It seemed so formal and such a grown-up thing to do. We settled in there and started the process of getting married. My Uncle David lived not far from our wee room. He was the 'black sheep' of Dad's family and I had heard many a story about his antics with drink and women! We got to know the area and the locals quite quickly through my uncle, because he had lived in the area for many years. My cousin Michael took us to where we could get speed and hash, so that was us all set up for our happy-ever-after life!

The Ibrox, Govan area of Glasgow was a hotbed of drunks, and I saw a lot of violence in the streets and the pubs. One night in particular, we were with my uncle in the pub when the doors burst in and a pile of guys all with weapons came charging in shouting and roaring someone's name. Frighteningly, he was sitting quite near me. One of the guys swiped at him with a sword as he jumped up trying to get away – he got away through the lounge, but his ear was still with us in the bar!

We set a date for our wedding in October of that year. I would be 19 by then. I was happily preparing for the wedding from our wee room in Cessnock. I would love to say that we were planning and preparing together, but that wouldn't be true. I think in the fog of drink and drugs, Simon didn't really get into the preparing part of it. I think I was excited because it seemed such a grown-up thing. My aunt took me out to look for shoes to go with the blue and pink flowery dress I had bought. I knew I couldn't really get away with the white wedding thing; I might have met what I thought was my hero, saviour etc, but I knew fairy tale endings were not for me.

The first time Simon lost his temper with me was in the summer of that year. We had been in the room in Cessnock for a few weeks and were just settling in to knowing each other in a semi-stable environment. I heard a band coming down Paisley Road West and flung the window up to wave at it. The next thing I knew, Simon grabbed my hair and threw me onto the floor, punched me in the face and told me never to do that again. I was completely confused. Of all the things to get angry about, why was he angry about me waving at the bands? Later on, when I felt it was safe to broach the subject, I asked him to tell me what I had done wrong. He explained about the Catholic-Protestant thing and that what I thought was the floats for the local fair was a sectarian march for Protestants. It was called an Orange Walk. I was to learn a lot more about the Orange Walks as time went on.

After all I had been through, I just kind of accepted I had done something wrong and it wouldn't happen again.

How naïve – of course it was going to happen again. And again, for that matter.

Time moved on and so did we, from one horrible room to another. We kept getting moved on for unsociable behaviour: being drunk and fighting and the likes.

We got a little room in Ibrox which wasn't too bad; the landlady was just as unsociable as us! She was an older lady who was full of fun and happy to spend her money on drink for us. She would come to the door late at night dressed up to go play tennis or something, and ask if we wanted to share her carry out. One night she asked us over to her house for dinner and drinks. I was thinking that maybe we had made it to another level! Jean was as bubbly as usual and pouring out drink like there was no tomorrow. Eventually I had had enough and staggered up the stairs to my bed. After a couple of hours, I realised Simon was still drinking downstairs. I went down to get him and another drink, and there they were, at it in full Technicolor glory. I wasn't sure what to do; so much was hammering through my head. She was our landlady, so we could end up out on the streets. I had had enough punches from Simon to know that doing anything about it might set the two of them on me. I slowly turned around and walked upstairs again with my heart pounding in my ears. I was in pain but didn't know how to deal with it. *Do I leave him? Do I confront him sober? Do I say nothing but refuse to go near her house again?*

What? What? What? In the end I said nothing, but the pictures of them at it burned in my mind for a long time. I reasoned with myself that, measuring what I had just witnessed with what I had been through, it wasn't really that bad. At least they hadn't asked me to join them! Simon and I both watched hardcore porn quite often and I thought that maybe he just needed a bit more.

Eventually we got a council flat on the 19th floor of a block of flats in Broomloan Road. I was overjoyed on two counts. One, this was my first home; a real house that was all mine and we didn't have to share it with anyone! Two, there was no more Jean. I knew they had been at it quite a lot and was glad to leave her smelly rented rooms! The flats were grey, damp-looking buildings, but I didn't really care: it was going to be our home. The flat had three bedrooms; perfect to start a family. We moved in with nothing at all. We put all our clothes in the smallest room and made a makeshift bed out of them. The DHSS gave us grants and a new bed, new cooker and new fridge. It was fun making our new home. Simon even got a job selling the *Daily Record* on the street at night, which helped to fund our growing drug and drink problem.

Now that we had a house, we could start a family. Until this point, my only pregnancy had been the one so viciously ended by Mick. I had never used any form of contraception, so as time went by and there was no sign of a pregnancy, we decided to go to the doctor to see if anything was wrong. We were put in touch with the relevant hospital and tests began as to why we were not conceiving. Every test in the book was done on both of us, and it was decided the reason we were not conceiving was unexplained infertility. I probably could have explained it, no problem! The issue of me not being able to have children was something he would bring up at every opportunity. It became a wedge between us.

We carried on with life, and met a couple called Sharon and Giovanni. They were both heavy drug addicts into heroin and anything else they could get their hands on. I really liked Sharon; we became friends and were introduced to a load of other people that were hooked on heroin and other drugs. We dabbled in that area but never really got in that deep. Sharon was a practising Buddhist and started telling me how good it was at helping you to get in touch with yourself and deep into areas of healing by chanting and saying some Japanese words out of a book. I went along to some of the meetings and got right into it. I had my own butsudan and gohonzon and beads, the lot. I faithfully chanted to the east with my greenery etc. Sharon and I became firm friends, through this and our love for Eldorado wine! Eventually, things went sour between Giovanni and Sharon. He left her on her own with two small kids and a habit. I helped out as much as I could, but was facing my own demons with the problems I had with Simon and his temper. I could hardly breathe and he would be complaining. My hero had since dropped down to zero.

I was enjoying the Buddhism stuff but had an unusual experience that put me right off it. I clearly remember one sunny summer day and I had been chanting for ages in my bedroom. I distinctly heard a voice say to me, "I don't want you to do that any more." I jumped up and looked out the window to see who said it. I thought it might have been some of the young lads passing by the window, but there was no one there at all. In any direction I looked, I could see no one! I felt a sudden shot of fear. I shut the box, put it in a bag, took it back to Sharon and told her I would not be going to the meetings any more. I got such a fright and was not comfortable having the box in my room. I can't even say I missed it all. It just wasn't for me, but I think having something nice in common with someone was a good feeling.

We moved on from that phase and got on with life in general. It soon became clear Simon had a problem with his temper when he was drunk, which was often. I had many a black eye or bruised rib as we went on.

One night, when Simon was out selling the *Daily Record*, I set our bedroom on fire accidentally with a heater that was placed too near a nylon bedspread. Our bedroom was gutted and we lost a lot of our clothes. I put in for a move out of the flats after that because I was so scared at being 19 floors up and trapped in a burning flat. We got a swap with a family with children that needed the three bedrooms, and we took their two-bedroom flat in an area of Govan called wine alley. It was so called because it had a really bad reputation for alcohol abuse and drugs. Simon became a regular at the local pub. We were regularly getting drunk and fighting. Simon got into loads of bother at the local pub; he would start trouble with Rangers fans because he was a Catholic and a Celtic fan. It was terrible sometimes.

We bought a Rottweiler as a guard dog to help keep us safe because Simon was always getting threatened. I can recall more than one occasion when I opened the door to guys with baseball bats or knives. Simon often spent the night in the cells in Govan until he cooled off.

I decided to leave him after one really nasty clash when he started fighting with me over nothing in particular. I started to fight back and he threw me over the sofa and was about to smash my face in with a pan when my neighbour kicked the door in and saved my life. After, I asked her why that time, out of all the times they must have heard us fighting, did she kick the door in? She just said it sounded different and she felt she had to do something. I am thankful to this day that she did.

I headed off home yet again to Mum's house, and went from there to a job in Inchinnan near Glasgow airport. I was a nanny again, which was hilarious, to a young boy named Tony. I settled in there well. I knew the score: housework and anything else distasteful that was my job, and mind the child, who was old enough to look after himself really. I soon got to know many of the locals, most of them intimately! I was so confused about who I was and what I was supposed to be that I would go looking for sex to comfort myself, knowing somebody had liked me in that moment. I was a sad, confused and lonely young woman on the inside.

At that point, I decided it was time to find out where I came from. I knew only a few facts: that I had an older sister and my natural parent obviously didn't want me. I phoned the registrar in Edinburgh to make an appointment to see my birth certificate. I was so nervous. I didn't know how I was going to feel seeing that it really was true. Sometimes it's easy to try to kid yourself it's not true, that really you're not adopted and it was just a story. I often wished that was true; I didn't like being adopted. I even got dressed nicely to go to the registrar, thinking that might make some kind of difference to the information it may carry.

When I got there, I struggled to go to the desk and say I was there to see my birth certificate. Eventually, I found myself in this very austere-looking room with a guy who was carrying a massive book with my birth certificate in it. When he opened it, I could hardly breathe with the tension I felt. I looked and looked at the page but I couldn't really see the writing at first. Then the guy pointed out to me where my parent's name was; I was stunned there was only one parent. Immediately, I started thinking, *oh my goodness, this is bad. Now I still don't know where I come from. I have to find this woman and see who my other parent is.* The guy politely asked me if he could assist me any further, and let me know what the price of a copy of the birth certificate would be. I declined his offer to buy a copy, as I felt I had all I needed and didn't really want to be reminded daily that I was an adopted child. I went back to where I was living and cried for such a long time. I don't really know what I was crying about, but I knew I had just opened up a huge can of worms in my heart.

The next day, I was digesting the information I had written down that was on the birth certificate. I phoned Mum and Dad. Dad knew of the village where I had been born and told me if I called the Forestry Commission in the area they may have a record of where the family had gone. It almost seemed too easy. My heart was in my mouth. I swithered and dithered all day about *will I or won't I?* Eventually, I did call the Forestry Commission, and they knew straight away who the family were. They were able to tell me it had been a man called Hugh and his wife Jessie that had been at that address, and that Hugh had died quite some time ago, but Jessie now lived in another village not that far away from Glentrool.

I came off the phone in a daze. It all seemed far too easy. I went home and discussed all the implications with Mum and Dad. They were happy for me to go ahead and find out what I could if it was going to help me settle down. I had already spoken to social workers about all the possible scenarios of how I would feel if she was dead or didn't want me to see her, or even how would I feel if she embraced me with open arms like nothing ever happened. It was all very emotional and scary. The options were humungous. What would I feel and how would it affect me if she was dead?

The next day, I went to directory enquiries and asked for the phone numbers of all the Kirkpatricks in that particular village. There were a few of them, as it is a very common name in the borders. I called one or two and they didn't know Jessie. The third one I called knew who Jessie was and asked me to call back in 10 minutes while she went and got her to come to the phone. Without really thinking about how she would feel, I just let her go and get her. I was about to speak to my natural granny, my natural mum's mum. In a flash, I suddenly realised I was completely unprepared for the news she may be dead or, worse, was alive and didn't want to see me. The fear factor was unreal. What would I even say?

"Hello," I heard this tiny, frail voice saying to me. "Hello, hello." I was stumped for something to say; my ears were ringing with fear and my heart was thumping with nerves. "Hello," I said back, "this is Helen, Margaret's daughter." I heard a gasp and a little cry. I realised then that must be quite shocking for an elderly lady to just suddenly hear. Someone took the phone from her and asked me what was going on. I tried to explain as well as I could. Jessie then came back on the phone, very tearful and trying to tell me 20-plus years of news in one go! My head was melting. My heart was on overdrive.

I phoned a couple of days later to get Margaret's address, to write to her. I knew she didn't want to give me up, but she had to. I also knew my aunt had also cared for me before I was given away. I was so excited about all this new information about who I was. I thought, at last, I had found the answer to my insecurities and fears. How stupid was I?

I got in touch with Simon to let him know I had found my natural "mum" and I was going to move to London to get to know her a bit better. Would he like to come with me? We could have a fresh start. We moved to London together and rented a room in a house close to Maggie, as I had decided to call her. We were soon introduced to my sisters, Lynne and Dorothy. Lynne was so like me, it was incredible. Dorothy was quick to tell me she was struggling with the whole idea, but we could get to know each other slowly. I had a brother, Eric, who was just about to turn 18. He was friendly, but not that interested in me as a sister. Things with Simon were OK; he seemed to be settling back into London all right and was not so angry all the time.

My drug use had evened out to smoking hash and having the odd line of speed. I loved a drink, though, and could drink a fair amount. Maggie was an expert drinker and had been in and out of psychiatric units with her own addiction to alcohol. She had been very violent as a younger woman with the drink. Lynne, Dorothy and especially Eric, started to share some horrible stories of what they had to endure and see as young children. I was glad then of my good childhood and upbringing.

We were all happily getting on with life in London. There were some ups and downs, but all seemed well. Lynne was having real problems with her partner, who was extremely violent and abusive when he had been drinking and taking drugs. Many a time we had to rescue Lynne and her two small kids from his attacks.

Out of the blue one morning, Lynne came and told me she had slept with Simon and they were getting together. When I confronted him about it, he said his reason for moving in with Lynne was that he wanted children, and with Lynne he could have them. I still had not conceived during all this time. I was shocked and hurt. I knew Lynne was jumping out of the fire with her partner and into the frying pan with Simon. Sure enough, not long after they moved in together, he hit her with a plant pot. I couldn't really get my head round it all, and moved to a house that my brother was staying in with a gay couple, Maxine and her partner.

I realised my drinking was totally out of control, and I was doing things I would later regret. More than once I woke up in Maxine's bed. That's when I decided to go to my aunt's flat in the Gorbals. This is where, feeling so lonely, exhausted and finished at 22 years old, I attempted to end my life.

After my failed attempt at killing myself, I realised I didn't want to die, but I also didn't want to go back to anything I had been involved with. The pornography that I had been exposed to as a child had been a strong influence all the way through my relationships and, in particular, with Simon. We had even sent some DIY shots to some mags.

I applied for a flat in Glasgow and was allocated one in the scheme that I had lived in with Simon. I felt safer there, where people knew who I was. There was a guy on my landing that sold hash, so I didn't really have to go anywhere to get drugs either. I just spent my time in other people's houses getting smashed. It seemed OK to me. No one was bothering me, and I wasn't bothering anyone. All was well. I got a little runt of a puppy free from someone in the scheme and called it Lily. Lily was a bad idea; I didn't have the first clue about training a puppy to do the toilet outside, so it pooed all around the house, which wasn't too bad as I only lived in one room of the house and didn't really have any stuff. That poor puppy was full of fleas and got taken to the police station at Govan and handed in as a stray. I had to get the council to spray the place; the fleas were jumping up people's legs when they came in!

I met my second husband, Tam, a few weeks later. He was the guy that was selling the hash on my landing. He asked me in one night and we chatted away for hours. He had been through some stuff as well. After a while, he moved in to my flat and we got on fine. My addiction to drugs was stable in as much as it was manageable, and my addiction to pornography was fuelled by Tam's love for it as well. We got on well together. I felt I had made it to some level of almost normality, in my twisted view of what life was supposed to be like.

Tam had a few brothers, and one called Alec, who was inside for attempted murder. When it was Tam's turn to visit him, he asked if I would pose as Alec's girlfriend and pass him drugs through kissing. I thought, *why not?* It was quite easy to do, and we did it a few times, sometimes changing our tactics. We would take one of his kids and put the drugs around the baby, or drop the package into the tea if it was an open visit. On one memorable occasion, I remember slipping the package into the tea and, lo and behold, it floated to the top. I was staring at Alec to get him to notice it and get rid of it quickly; I couldn't do it because I had put the tea in front of him and I was at the other side of the table. I had visions of being arrested and marched out in front of everyone! Luckily, Alec caught on to what happened and got rid of it fast. I have to tell you, at this point in my life, my father was a senior prison officer in another prison. The shame that would have brought on him at work was not even measurable.

We got news our scheme was getting pulled down to make way for some industrial units, so we decided to move to Falkirk, where most of my family were living. We got a little bed and breakfast room paid for by the social until we got a one-bed flat in what was quite possibly the worst street in Falkirk! Life in all its supposed state of normality consisted of getting up, having some speed, going out to buy drink, or sign on, or pretend to look for a job, come home, smoke some hash and drink the drink! Many a time we had nothing but toast to eat, to pay for our habit. Now and then we would get the odd bit of casual work or even a real job, but it never lasted long.

Tam and I tried for a baby for years and then began to have fertility treatment. We had every test in the book and, again, it came back as unexplained infertility. The hospital put us on the list for IVF treatment, and soon we were on the programme for that. Around the same time, my sister fell pregnant with her second child, but unfortunately he had spina bifida and was stillborn.

This was a huge turning point in my life as, a few months before, I had started having small seizures, which then became massive seizures. I had been hospitalised and told by the doctors that if I didn't stop drinking and taking drugs, my next seizure could be my last. I can vividly remember thinking to myself, what would happen when I was dead? *Do I just melt into the earth?* I was afraid that night, as I had just come face to face with the realisation that I was going to die. There was no way round it, even if it wasn't tomorrow or next week with a seizure, it was certainly something I wasn't going to get out of!

I started to think about what came next. I knew of lots of theories about reincarnation and I was very aware there was a world of the dead, because I had a few times seen spirits and people who were dead.

Ann Borland moved into our street. I don't know when she moved in, but I do remember seeing her marching across her living room regularly, going back and forward. Tam and I just thought she was a loony, like many of us that lived in the street! Ann, on the other hand, was a born-again Christian who had moved into the street and was praying for many of the messed-up residents. She says she used to pray regularly into our windows because she saw so many people coming and going from our block, and she had seen me being arrested a couple of times. Ann was praying and things were happening.

Tam and I had settled into a wee routine of getting up and having a puff and a line of speed. I went off to work in my brother's burger van some days, and I had a part-time job in the fruit and veg section of the local supermarket. One fine day, we received a letter from the hospital in Edinburgh. It was our turn to have a go at IVF treatment. Off we went for Tam to give them some sperm and for me to be given a nasal spray to boost my hormones.

It was at this time that I asked Ann, a bit randomly, if she went to a church, as things had been playing on my mind. The death of my nephew and years of abuse and the threat of death through that abuse had brought me to a place of searching. Ann quite happily told me all about The Peoples Church in Falkirk. I can remember thinking it was, A) A strange name for a church. Should they not be called saint something or another? And B) It was on, on a Sunday night! I was completely unaware that churches had services on a Sunday night. This church had their service in the morning and the one in the evening was more relaxed, and designed to bring visitors to. Ann was happy to call in for me the following Sunday night. At this point, I was just about at the end of the nasal spray part of my IVF, and hormones were clashing off each other. It was such a strange time, with so much happening all at once.

As we came in through the front door, a suited and booted young man politely shook my hand and welcomed us in. Next, there was an older lady standing in the hallway with a table and a big black book. Ann introduced me as being new and it being my first time. The lady scooped me into her ample bosom and, dare I say, gravy-stained white jumper, and hugged me! I was a bit taken aback; hugging people was not really my thing, especially a stranger, but I duly did as I was told and put my name and address in the book.

Ann then walked me into the church hall. The first thing I noticed was it was nice and bright with chairs and music and lots of people chatting and laughing with each other. This really wasn't my interpretation of church. The band struck up and everyone started to sing and clap. It was very noisy and felt fairly exciting.

I can't remember what the pastor was talking about at all. At the end of his sermon, he asked if there was anyone who would like to give their lives to Jesus. "Just put your hand up and we will pray for you," he said. I was getting very uncomfortable, feeling like I wanted to put my hand up, but feeling there was no way God/Jesus would want anyone like me. I started to sweat and stuck my hands under my bum in case they went up. I was totally convinced it was the massive amounts of hormones that were making me feel like that.

When the service was finished, people came up and said hello. It was all very friendly and nice. Ann seemed to know a lot of people in the church. We walked home and Ann asked me if I liked the service? I said I thought it was OK and thanks for taking me. When I got home, I was quite tired, and my husband was waiting to get stuck into the drink. We had a drink and I went to bed. I did think to myself that I wanted to go back to church once the IVF treatment was over.

Around this time, I met a lady called Jane at an Ann Summers party and signed up to be a rep. I had a few parties and seemed to be quite good at it. I made quite a bit of money having big parties, and won a few prizes at the meetings.

We continued with the fertility treatment. The next stage was a series of daily injections to bring my ovaries to bursting point with eggs. I really didn't like the daily injections at all. Soon it was time to go into hospital to have the eggs harvested. It sounds horrible, and I can assure you it was horrible. I was really sick with the anaesthetic and fainted in the car park when I got out. We were called back in a few weeks to see our newly conceived, outside-the-womb children. There were eight fertilised eggs in total and we were taken into a room and asked to choose two of them to be planted back into my womb. It was a very strange process; I truly didn't like any of it. Off we went home with my newly planted, fertilised eggs. After three weeks we went back for a pregnancy test, and all was well. I was working during the day at the fruit and veg stall and some evenings selling Ann Summers products.

It was a Tuesday afternoon. I was standing at the till in the fruit and veg shop when I felt a sensation of bleeding. I went off to the toilets and, sure enough, there was blood. I took off right out of the shop and went home as fast as I could. I lay on the couch willing it to go away, but another visit to the toilet showed me there was a real chance I was losing my babies. All night long, I was crying and going back and forth to the toilet. By morning it was over and we were both exhausted, physically and emotionally. I had to go back to the hospital, but I refused point-blank to go near the place again. They sent letters about the other embryos and follow-up treatment. They called and tried to speak to me, but I was determined I would not face such a painful thing ever again. I never went back.

The sense of loss for me was bigger than I expected. I had always longed for a child, hoping that it would fill the chasm of emptiness and lack of connection I always carried around with me. The disappointment was something that was too big for me to deal with. I just shined it on, as the saying goes.

By the Saturday of that week, I thought about The Peoples Church again and wondered, if I went back now that I was off the hormones and all the treatment, if I would feel anything like I had before? I went along on the Sunday night again with Ann and, this time, Tam decided to join me. When the pastor made an appeal for anyone to accept Jesus, my hand went straight up. I just knew, somewhere deep inside, that was what I had to do. Tam put his hand up too and we both went down the front and were prayed for, and it was explained to us what we had done. We were 'saved', as people kept telling us.

It was weird. I totally knew that something had most definitely happened to me and things were changing inside. I went to the Sunday services at church and enjoyed them, and started to go to the Tuesday Bible study and the Thursday prayer meetings. Ann bought me a Bible and a lady called Nora was assigned to be my mentor. Nora was a great example, and took me right under her wing. She encouraged me and helped me by being there through the ups and downs I was having with Tam. Tam wasn't getting it at all. He didn't really change and he didn't really have an experience with God or, if he did, he never did anything with it, or maybe he didn't know what to think or do about it. Nora was an absolute tower of strength. A powerhouse of prayer.

On the other hand, I did get it. I knew that God was real. I knew that Jesus died for my sins and that I had accepted Him as my saviour. The problem was I had so much to learn and even more to unlearn! I found it very hard to see where I fitted into the church. It was full of very nice people who were all well dressed and looked well-to-do. A few people did speak to me and made me feel welcome. I joined the discovery class and learned a few of the basics in Christianity like baptism, praying, the Bible basics. I loved those classes. They were good for me and I went to all ten of them; it was good to meet the other novices in the church, so then I didn't feel too much like I was the only one that didn't know what to do or say. I was beginning to fit in.

One evening it was announced that there was a 9.30 a.m. prayer meeting every weekday that was open to anyone to come and pray for an hour. I thought to myself I would like to have gone to that. I started to attend it and met a few women around my age that were helping with the cleaning. There was also a woman called Margaret Hunter who kept us all right with the cleaning duties. Margaret was very quietly spoken and from up north;

she had a beautiful voice that was so gentle and soothing. Beneath the voice was a woman of determination and steel. I grew to love Margaret very deeply; she was such a woman of wisdom. I loved going to her beautifully clean house and having tea and a sandwich. She would patiently answer any of my million and one questions and instil in me the need to read my Bible and pray. Her husband Robert was a gem; a great storyteller and so, so funny and endlessly patient. He was quite hard of hearing and I would always wonder how on earth they communicated, as Margaret was so softly spoken and never came across as someone who would shout. I very often thought about how amazing it was that these nice, good, kind people would let someone like me sit in their house.

Nora, my mentor, was probably the biggest influence in my Christian life. She had been assigned to me and I liked her straight away. Nora had been a Christian for a few years, and had four children who were all in the church as well. Her husband, Bryan, didn't attend really. We would walk to the church together or get the bus, and she would always share her great stories with me about what was going on in the family. She had a brilliant family life. Nora was always there for me. Any time I didn't get something, she would painstakingly explain it to me. She would get me in her kitchen and tell me off nicely, explaining that God didn't really want us to be doing whatever it was I was doing. I didn't quite get it all at once.

I made friends with other people in the church and started being invited round to people's houses, which was nice. Some of the people I made friends with were not such a good example as Nora or Margaret, I have to say, and I got drawn into gossip and bad ways that were not really what I thought good people were supposed to be doing. I had this common misconception that Christians were good all the time. I can remember one time being in this Bible class after church one Sunday. The class was fine, but the teachers were always making smart remarks about the pastor. It started to make me feel uncomfortable, because I knew that he had not done anything to me and I kind of thought that if he had upset these folks, then maybe they should talk to him, instead of letting us all hear it. I went to the church one Sunday and one of the teachers approached me with a piece of paper to sign. I asked what it was and they just said, "Oh, you just have to sign it." I read it, and it was basically a petition to have something the pastor had been trying to put in place disagreed with. I was fuming that they thought I would just sign the thing without even telling me what it was. I shoved the paper right back at the guy and told him where to shove his bit of paper. God still had a lot of work to do in me!

I began to get involved in different areas of the church, like the cleaning and the coffee morning, and made sure I attended all the classes, like the discovery class and the Sunday Bible class. I enjoyed learning about God and how His son Jesus had died on the cross for me. I didn't really fully understand it all, but I knew I had been touched by something bigger than me.

So much within me needed fixing that I began to despair of how on earth God would be able to fix all the stuff that was going on in my heart and mind. So much had happened to me. So many times I had been in situations where I had chosen quite specifically to do the wrong thing. What was it going to take to sort all that out?

I had been attending the church for a while, trying to work it all out and really getting nowhere fast. I had a Bible that I read from cover to cover and back again, and had begun to pray and ask God to help me to understand some of this stuff. It was all so unfamiliar. Nothing in church was familiar to me, and I was uncomfortable there. I was uncomfortable with the majority of the people. In my opinion, everyone was good and kind and nice and I was bad and ugly and not nice. This is not a reflection on the people in the church; it's more of a reflection of where I was at and my lack of understanding.

So, as I went on day by day trying to get a grip of what was happening in my life and in my heart, my life was slowly changing but I was unaware of it. Other people would say to me that I was doing well and looking well, but I couldn't see it myself.

As time was going on and I was praying, reading and getting to know about God, unfortunately my husband was not getting it, and I was really struggling to cope with me being one way and him being another. He was just behaving in the only way he knew how. He was still watching porn at night and taking drugs and alcohol. I continued to attend the church and didn't really share what was going on at home. If the truth be told, I didn't really know what to say about what was going on in my house. I know that I felt a sense of shame and was always feeling a bit worried that, because this was going on in my home, maybe God would not be coming to my house. That made me worry a little about how was I going to carry on.

Things got so bad that Tam would lock me out the house if I went to church on the Sunday morning, and not let me come home until after the evening service. I used to wander around Camelon, waiting until the service was starting at night. Once or twice, someone asked me to have dinner in their house.

One Sunday afternoon, I was wandering around and heard singing I recognised as one of the songs we sang at the church. I went into the building that the song was coming out of and found a church called Victory Outreach, who were having a couple of songs before they ate their Sunday meal. There was a crowd of real strange-looking characters all sitting or standing around in a big hall. Someone came to speak to me and asked if I needed help? I just said I had heard a song I recognised and was hanging around until my church started at 6.30 p.m. It was so welcoming, and I felt really at home. I was introduced to the minister and his wife, Mike and Joanne. They were so lovely. I felt quite at home when I found out most of the men and women were ex-drug addicts, and part of what they called The Home, where the men lived in one home and the women in another. The church was beginning to establish itself in the community. I was amazed at the homes and the testimonies of the people that were there: ex-heroin addicts, alcoholics and prostitutes all living together and worshipping the Lord. One of the things that made me chuckle was the pastor was an ex-policeman. I went there every Sunday that I needed to, to get fed and have somewhere to go between services at my own church. I wondered what it would be like to go to this church instead. I did speak to a couple of the women in my own church about it and they suggested I should just stick with the church I was in, as I was such a new Christian, and moving churches might not be helpful in my growth.

I still went round to spend time with a lady called Tracey, who was running the women's home. I was intrigued by what she was doing by taking women straight from the streets into her home and detoxing them, then teaching them to get and keep a relationship with Jesus.

Tam was still in a place where he was not understanding anything about the church or God or what was happening to me. He did try to get it, but he just could not get the concept into his head of there being an enemy. Eventually our marriage crumbled and, no matter how much I prayed and tried to make it work, things got to the point where he left me for another woman. We had even gone away to a caravan for a break to see if that would help. He just didn't understand it all or what had happened to me. While we were away, fuelled with alcohol, he shoved my back hard into a bush and yelled in my face that he wanted the old me back. The old me was slowly receding and the new me was blossoming out of all the years of pain, hurt, betrayal, drugs and alcohol. As it turned out, he had been having an affair for a while with a woman he worked with. She was pregnant, giving him the one thing I never could.

I had been away, staying over with a friend and, after the early morning prayer meeting, I made my way home. I knew as soon as I opened the door that things were not as they should be. My bed was gone and the gorgeous pink shiny bedspread that I loved and he hated was lying where the bed should have been. It was so painful that day to come home and find he had gone, and had taken some of our things with him. How dare he. I mean, OK, take off with this woman and do the right thing by the child, but taking our bed and washing machine and a few other essentials was real low behaviour. I didn't really understand the fact he had gone. I couldn't really understand why he had gone, either, because as far as I was concerned, I had gone from being a complete mess as a wife to being almost the Stepford wife. So, why on earth would he prefer to be with someone who was a mess?

I struggled to deal with being on my own at first, and realised that because he was gone, I really couldn't keep the flat on, as I couldn't pay the rent or any of the bills on my own. I had to give up the flat, and found myself on my own and homeless with little or no income. Thankfully, there was a woman in the church that took me in to her house and let me stay there until I got myself somewhere to stay.

God really started to show me what He was capable of in that time. I started to pray for a place of my own.

Although where I was staying was great, it was not ideal, and I knew I had to move on. Being on my own and in a very quiet house with a disabled lady who lived on her own was the perfect place for me to be at that time. It was like a little incubation pod. My relationship with God was beginning to grow, and I had excessive time to pray, read, sing, and study the Bible. I had struggled in the beginning of my walk, as all I knew for sure was that something had most certainly touched me. The song that I loved at the time was *He Touched Me*. I was getting more involved in the church and all that went on; helping to clean, working in the coffee morning, being on the welcome team. I was always really aware of what I was wearing on the welcome team. I could never get that vision of the huge bust with the gravy stain coming to get me in a hug on my first visit to The Peoples Church. I want to mention a wonderful man called John Ferguson, our welcome team leader, and his love, understanding and way of pouring cold water on my complaints and mumblings.

Pastor George McKim and his wife Linda were so supportive and helpful in this season. I will always be grateful to them, as long as I live. George was always available and on hand to talk to and, many times, I was able to pour out my heart and ask him why things had been so awful, and why God allowed such things to happen to me. There are things to this day that only George McKim knows about my life. His acceptance of me, warts and all, was a real turning point for me in my journey. I had felt sure that, once he knew what I had been like, he would not want me in the church at all.

It has to be said at this point that, when you go into church and have that experience of coming to know and accept Christ as your saviour, knowing and understanding that God is completely real, you know what has happened to you is not of your own doing, not willpower, not coercion, etc. As an ex-drug addict, thief, liar, immoral person, going into an environment where you feel completely alien is incredibly difficult. I felt in the beginning that people were moving their bags away from me, when in reality they were moving them under the seat so I didn't fall over and smash my face on the floor as I squeezed past to get into a seat in a row of chairs. It felt to me that the majority of people didn't want to talk to me because I was what I was. In reality, what people were seeing was a strange individual growling at anyone that looked squint at me. God had so much work to do in me. I felt I was not good enough for God or to be around these good people. It was a difficult time. The discovery class brought a level of inclusion quickly, while teaching me the basics.

I still needed a place to live. I was praying daily to God for a house. I wasn't really too fussed on what type of house; I just needed to settle on my own. I bugged the council daily. It was before the days of mobile phones, and where I was staying didn't even have a landline I could use. I had given the church office number as my point of contact, and I was there every day cleaning and at the daily prayer meetings. Pastor David the assistant minister at the time called me through for a phone call one day. It was the council. Was I free that day to go look at a prospective property in Hallglen? "Absolutely," I said, "when do you want me there?" The house was mine; a two-bed house on the end of a row in Hallglen. I was delighted, and also in a state of shock. It had all happened so fast. I didn't even have so much as a chair to sit on.

Amazingly, my house was filled with stuff in no time. The word had gone out to some of the women and so much happened so quickly; people were arriving at my door with TVs, beds, kitchen things, bedding, etc. Some people gave me money to buy the things I didn't have. After the whirlwind of moving into the house had died down, I realised I was in a house on my own, stone cold sober. Wow. That in itself was quite a miracle. It was fine for a bit but, after a while, I didn't really like being on my own. I began to experience real fear of being attacked in my own home. I was paranoid at every tiny sound. My doors were always locked and the windows were shut tight at night. Where was God now? I wasn't exactly sure at that point.

So much had happened. Mum had gone through a brain aneurysm and almost died. She had been visiting the church before it and pastor David had gone to the hospital and prayed for her. She survived two bursts and a torsion bleed behind her eyes which left her almost blind for a long time. Dad had died suddenly from a blood clot. Although I had grown in my walk with God, knew how to pray, knew to read my Bible, all of a sudden, on my own, I wasn't as keen to read and pray. I started missing the morning prayers and the odd Tuesday Bible study night and Thursday prayer night. My wax was waning.

The fears and insecurities started to build up and I felt I was being strangled all the time. *This can't be right? Why do I feel like this?* I felt lonely and left out, rejected, abandoned, unwanted. All the old memories came flooding in. *You're not a Christian. Those people don't like you. They are just using you to clean the church and do the errands for them. Where are they now that you're on your own feeling like this?*

I tried to explain what was going on, but just felt stupid and awkward saying it. Nora was great. She would have me over and pray for me over my cheese and mayonnaise sandwich. Even now, 25 years later, on a down day I still crave one of Nora's cheese and mayonnaise sandwiches, with prayer, of course.

It all came to a head one day at church. A couple of women were annoying me. Oh yes, Christians get annoyed. I had an argument with one of them and stormed off, absolutely raging. It was over. This Christian thing was not for me; too many hypocrites, too many people I didn't like or deem fit to be Christians. I got myself a beautiful bottle of cheap wine and headed home to my miserable, lonely house. The first glass of it was horrible, but I kept going anyway. My phone in the hallway was ringing, but I was ignoring it. I knew I shouldn't be drinking, but was on a mission. After a while, there wasn't much left in the bottle, and I was still fuming. I decided to let a few people know how I actually felt about them. Drunk, I started dialling numbers and letting rip, full of booze, at the poor people who answered their phones. I was quite enjoying myself; it felt great to me.

The next thing I knew, my door was banging and my windows were getting knocked on. It was two of the older women from the church, one of whom had been on the receiving end of a tirade. In they came and promptly took the new bottle of booze I had just got from the shop off me, and sat me down to try to sober me up. They stayed for hours, giving me food and tea to drink. They prayed for me, hugged me, told me it was OK, that these things happen, move on from it. I thought for sure I was obviously not a Christian any more. I was still to learn about the grace and love of

Christ. I was a judgemental, hard Christian with no understanding of grace and mercy, until I needed some myself. I thought I could never set foot on the hallowed ground of the church ever again.

My friends were great. There was no judgement: only love and understanding. Some even shared their own stories where they had fallen into temptation in various ways. To hear that these good people were not as perfect as their houses and clothes would have me believe was a real game changer for me. We all fall short ...

So many things to deal with, and so much was still new to me. Life happens, whether you're a Christian or not. I had to continue to go to church, to continue to learn to read my Bible. Prayer was a key I had still so much to learn about. My keys at this time going forward were my Bible, reading it, studying it, singing – I actually love singing and prayer. My keys a couple of years back were drugs and alcohol. I had to learn not to default back to that and move on from the blip.

The first Sunday I went back to church, I felt awful. I sat at the back. Why do we do that when we are feeling bad? It was Communion time; something that happened every Sunday. I knew I was unfit to take it because of what I had done. I passed the thing on when it came to me. After Communion, one of the male elders that gave Communion tapped me on the shoulder to come out with him. I thought for sure I was getting kicked out of the church. He asked me why I had passed over the Communion. I felt awful, bursting into tears as I explained what had happened during the week before. He was so kind, listening patiently through my tears. He gently held my hand and asked me if I was sorry about it. Of course I was sorry about it; I was dying of shame. I didn't want to make God unhappy. I loved Him. I knew what He had done for me. The elder led me to the kitchen where, on the counter, was one cup of wine and one piece of cracker sitting all by itself. He said to tell the Lord I was sorry and then take Communion. The door quietly shut and I was on my own with my bread and wine. That experience taught me more than any book, and I've never forgotten that lovely individual.

As time marched on and seasons followed seasons, my life continued to be filled with stuff. I prayed regularly and still attended church. I still went to the 6.30 a.m. prayer meeting and also the 9.30 a.m. prayer meeting. Getting to know people and beginning to put my trust in God, not people, was hard. I found it all really difficult. I didn't know who to trust, who to stick with. People are people whether they are Christians or not. Many times, I wanted to just walk away, being totally fed up with the things people in church were doing and saying. It was of course everyone else's fault. I began to feel bitter and resentful towards people who had let me down or who had done something unholy (as I saw it). I was still living under the impression that everyone in the four walls of the church was supposed to be good and kind and nice. I still had so much to learn about God's grace and mercy. I was learning, bit by bit, and it was becoming clearer. My judgemental little self was starting to soften.

I had been taking in women from the church who needed a bed for a season. Some just needed a bed for a couple of weeks, some needed longer-term stays, and one girl stayed over a couple of university terms. I enjoyed every one of them being in my house and learned a lot from each experience. Each woman had her own ways and each had her own relationship with God. I was learning so much about our own personal walk with God – not to compare and to try not to judge. Is that possible, not to judge others? I'm not too sure that little fiend ever really dies. My dream was to be able to work with women. I love women, and how hard we are to fathom. I knew how hard I had found it going to church and trying to be a Christian. I wanted to work towards being a woman who helps women. My house was a great tool in those days to have so many great characters come to stay.

I knew I needed a change. I also knew that I was going to work with women in the future, especially those that were addicted, as I had been. I needed to get my act together and start building my life up. I looked into going to college. There were a few courses I looked at, and I settled on a hospitality management HND. It had all the elements I believed I would need to set up a home for women who needed to be free from drugs and alcohol.

I continued to attend the 6.30 a.m. prayer and began my journey as a mature student at 34 years of age. The class was small; 14 started, I think. They were all very young, and the next oldest to me was 21, and the oddest bunch of people ever. I loved it. The teachers were great, the youngsters were great, and being a Christian in the midst of it all was very interesting. I was able to share what I believed and support some of the younger students in their own journeys through life. To this day, I still keep them in prayer and wonder where they are and what they are doing.

The course ended and I passed with a merit. I was as pleased as punch. During the time I was at the college, I had begun to date an older man from the church. He had asked me out and I accepted. It felt nice having male company again. He was nice and very flattering in the beginning. As the relationship went on, we got engaged and started to plan our wedding. Cracks began to appear in the relationship; all was not as it seemed. I was afraid to say anything, as he had been in the church for years and I felt I couldn't say anything. I started to really pray about this relationship, as we were fast approaching marriage. I felt the Lord telling me that he was not the one. I immediately felt fear. By this time I knew he was not going to be good for me and I was experiencing moments of fear around him, as he was very intense and a little controlling. I knew those feelings of fear. I had, of course, had them before. I knew it was going to end badly.

Seven weeks before the wedding date, I had to sit down with him and tell him the wedding was off. I knew that God had not chosen him for me. I was not going to marry him. To say that he took it badly is an understatement.

I moved into my sister's house for a short time as things were very difficult surrounding the break-up. He left the church. I continued to go, as I had been doing. I had done nothing wrong. My pastor took me aside one day not long after the break-up and said he had seen me becoming like a bird trapped in a cage as the relationship grew. I was gutted. *How could that have gone so wrong? Was I just flattered by the male attention, and not paying attention to the alarm bells?* We had become more intimate the closer it got to the wedding, which I thought wasn't too bad. We didn't have sex, but did get to know each other quite well. He was what I thought of as the perfect catch: handsome, clever, had his own house, a great job. But he was not who God was preparing for me.

My life needed filling again. I began to take women into my house again and had a variety of characters that helped me to take the focus off myself and get on with life. There was a real variety of women, most of whom were addicts in one shape or form. One young lady would come out of the bathroom regularly with hair green one day, striped the next. Every woman in that season, I still keep in prayer to this day.

By 2001, I had been saved nearly five years and was trotting along fairly well; certainly nowhere near perfect, and still learning all the time. The Peoples Church decided to launch a bus to reach out to the addicts in our town. We would go out and sit in the bus and, when people came on, we would share our stories and the stories of others with them. We had soup and tea and biscuits, but it was about soul-winning and bringing healing to others caught up in addiction. We met hundreds of addicts, young and old, some on heroin, others on crack cocaine, some alcoholics. We offered them Teen Challenge recovery homes or Victory Outreach Recovery Homes, to go to sort their lives out.

The team decided to do an official launch for the bus and to do a crusade inviting as many addicts and young people to church as we could. Victory Outreach London came up with a team of ex-addicts to help us go on the streets and into the schools with advice and testimonies of the wonderful things God had done.

The team were incredible, led by a newly licenced minister, Paul Lloyd. He had a team of men and women from the Victory Outreach Homes in London. They were on fire: up at the crack of dawn, praying, worshipping and preparing well for each day out on the streets. It was one of the most exciting things I had been involved in as a Christian at that point. I was enthralled by the testimonies, the discipline of the team. The camaraderie of the group was great to be a part of. I was very much enjoying being part of the team, serving them. The schools were blessed by their stories and so many people were touched by their stories on the streets

On the Tuesday night of the crusade, a young man had made his way to be fed at The Salvation Army where Paul Sinicki was volunteering. He spoke to all the people that were there that night and let them know The Addict Team was at The Peoples Church that night, and they were all welcome to go and hear some stories. A few did come down that night, and one of them was Brian Myles, a 21-year-old heroin addict. There was a preacher called George Miller speaking that night, on faith and going a little further. There were testimonies and one of them was by Andy Young, someone Brian had seen a few years ago when he was in the Victory Outreach Home in Falkirk. The transformation was amazing, and Andy was doing a good job of giving all the credit for his transformation to God. When it came time to do a call-out for people to make a decision on whether they would like to accept Jesus into their lives, there was a bit of an exodus of people leaving, but Brian and a few others stayed and made that decision. It was March the 6th, 2001, my 35th birthday. Brian made that decision by going down the front and being prayed for. My friend and mentor Nora chose him as someone we would continue to keep in prayer, as her husband was called Bryan too. As simply as that.

That night, Brian made the choice to put his trust in God and take the brave step to go down to London into the home. He was asked by the team to bring his coach fare in and they would book the bus the next day. He did, and off he went to London to begin his journey of faith in Christ.

The crusade was a huge success, and lots of people made the decision to give their lives to Christ. I was buzzing and totally on fire faith-wise. I had seen God do so much in so many lives in the space of a week. Lots of men had gone down to the home in London. It was now time to say goodbye to the team: Andy, Kenny, Sandra, Mandy, Gabrielle, Josie, Floyd, Dave and pastor Paul Lloyd. I wanted to go back with them to join their church and be a part of the work they were doing with the homes. I could have just packed up and gone, there and then, but I knew that was impulsive. I spoke to my pastor, and his advice was to wait until the hype died down, and see how I felt then. In the meantime, I could write to the people I had spent a fantastic week with. I chose to write to Josie, as her birthday had fallen in the week of the crusade, and I had got on with her so well. She had an incredible testimony as well.

Four months later, I was on a bus on my way to visit the homes to see how they worked and to see some of the people who had come down to the homes from the crusade. The visit was amazing. I spent some lovely times around the homes and met a couple of the men that had gone down. Brian was doing well; he had made a commitment to stay. While I was there, I spoke to the women's home director and asked if I could go down to spend a month in the home, as I really wanted to open my own house to female drug addicts, but with some sort of structure, not just living with me. It was arranged that I would go down about a month later. I was too excited. I really was looking forward to being in the home, learning about how it all worked and preparing myself to open my own house to women. I had a huge heart for women caught in addiction, and wanted so much for Scotland to have homes for addicts to go and get clean and find a relationship with God that would keep them, as He had kept me.

It was time to set off. I had just the minimum amount of stuff with me, as there wasn't a lot of space. I settled in well. I had no privileges, as I wanted to be in the same position as the women in the home. I needed to know what it felt like to not have the liberty to come and go as I pleased, to not have access to a phone or money, etc. I can tell you right now I did not like it one little bit! It started to get on my nerves being stuck in the same place and with the same people, not really getting any time to myself. The other women were getting on my nerves, noise was getting on my nerves. I love silence, but it was rarely even quiet in the home. There were two small children there as well, which added to my annoyance. They were lovely children but, as small children tend to do, they cried and carried on a lot, making loads of noise. I'm so not a fan of noise.

I learned so much in a very short space of time. I learned how to give a Bible study, how to lead prayer, and found out I was quite a good singer too. There was a great bond built with the people in the home, and the director, Cindy Punt, was a towering character, a powerhouse of talent and a real spiritual warrior. I was smitten with the whole thing. I loved the services and met so many incredible people. *This is me*, I kept saying to myself. *I'm meant to be here doing this.*

It was time to go back to Scotland (sad face). I threw myself into building up my house in Falkirk and had many characters come through my doors. Teen Challenge got in touch and asked if I would take in a phase four girl called Valerie. Phase four girls have finished the programme and are in the process of standing on their own two feet. She could help in the home with the ladies that were going in to detox, as that was quite hard work for one. I saw God heal many women, saw anorexia being healed, saw women healed of addiction and restored to their families. I took a few that I had detoxed off heroin to prepare for Teen Challenge down to Wales to begin their journeys of freedom. It was such a special time in my life.

I was loving it, but was still feeling that there was more for me. I was in prayer one morning and heard the Lord calling me to Victory Outreach. I was like, *what? Really?* I went to speak to my pastor again and told him I believed the Lord had called me to Victory Outreach. He was so understanding, and gave me his blessing to take the leap of faith to head off to the big smoke to start my new journey.

On the 6th of January, 2003, I landed in Victoria Station in London. Wow! I was really there, and there was Brian and his friend Barry waiting for me to get off the bus. They bundled me and my two cases into the back of a cab and off we went to the church.

The transition was very difficult for me; the whole lifestyle was not what I was used to. The pace of life was on warp speed 10 and I was coming from a gentle speed of three or three and a half. I was living with Cindy and her family, sharing a room with Josie that I had met on the crusade. She had graduated the home and was doing really well. It was a very busy house, with people always coming round and lots going on. Now remember, I love the quiet, and I'm not great in a crowd. After a month or so, I was looking for a job, as my meagre savings were running out fast. By this time, Brian, who had arrived from Falkirk, was working in a Christian bookshop called the Good News shop in Leyton. He asked his boss if I could get a job, and she took me on. It was amazing. I really enjoyed it, and was learning so much from Betty and her amazing faith. The job was hard work and good pay, and there was the bonus that Brian was there, so I didn't feel the odd one out. He looked after me very well. The journey to work was very long from Dagenham to Leyton and back again at night. I began to ask around for somewhere closer to the shop to live. A room came up in a Christian house within walking distance to the shop. Yes, count me in.

Things were going well. I was working, getting used to the new church. It was so different to what I was used to, and I was struggling with the change. They sang different songs, prayed out loud all at the same time, not politely waiting on the next person to pray. They were bold and fearless. Different people spoke from the pulpit; there were loads of pastors and it was confusing at first. I began to get used to it, but was struggling to connect with people. My own walk with Christ was waning as I was focusing again on how I was feeling. I struggle to connect at the best of times, even though God had done amazing work in my heart, and I no longer suffered from the feelings of rejection and abandonment, no longer felt ugly and unwanted. It had been a very long time since I felt lonely. I knew things were creeping back in. I felt lonely, different and out of the loop.

I missed my friends and family, my early morning daily prayer and cleaning the church. I felt I had no place in this church. I didn't have anyone really to talk to about how I was feeling. I prayed, of course I prayed. I read my Bible, did my devotions. But I missed having friends to talk to, to mull over how I was feeling, someone to have a laugh with. There was, of course, Brian at the shop, but he was young and not really someone I wanted to pour out my frustrations to. I was low and lonely; it felt like everyone was ignoring me. Church was miserable. I left most weeks on my own and walked home alone. I would go to the local Tesco and eat my dinner on my own. Don't get me wrong here, I like being on my own, but not all the time.

It had been said that when I went down to join VO, I would be working in the women's home with a view to being the next director. That didn't quite work out, as the home closed before I arrived, so there was an element of disappointment and, again, frustration at things not going as planned. I love working with women. I was passionate about women getting their lives free from all and any addiction. There were so many things I found women addicted to: drugs, drink, sex, shopping, food in a negative way, stealing, gambling and porn.

One addiction is not harder than the other to deal with; they are all just used to cover up 101 other issues. For me, rejection, abandonment and insecurity were three of the main things that took me down the roads of addiction.

It was Monday again, and off I went to work in the Good News shop in Leyton. Betty and Tom and their little dog Bethany were a great light in my life over this season of loneliness. Betty was a powerhouse of faith; she was messed about by nobody and her unwavering faith in Christ was incredible. Their testimony of salvation and how they turned the little cigarette shop into a flourishing, busy Bible book shop was inspiring. It had taken years of prayer and taking one step at a time, and there I was at a time when they were expanding into opening healing rooms above the shop. I loved learning all about the concept, the beginnings and being a part of the prayer team for the rooms opening.

I was just about to go for my lunch that day when I was called upstairs to take a phone call. It was Xavier from Teen Challenge. It was nice to hear from them; I had missed working with them detoxing women and having the phase four girls to stay when I was in Falkirk. He began to explain that they wanted to open a facility in

Ilford in London, and Paul Lloyd had recommended me as a candidate to take the position. It was live-in, well paid and everything that I had dreamed of. *Yes, yes, yes,* my head and heart screamed inside. No, no, no, the Holy Spirit said. What was going on? There was my ultimate dream come true being offered on a plate. Just before I left Scotland, I had been offered the position of women's facility manager in Teen Challenge Wales and had turned it down, confidently telling my pastor that I was called to Victory Outreach. There I was again, being offered the same, but now knowing there was no position for me in VO women's home. *Should I not just take it and see what happens?* Again the Holy Spirit was clearly saying no. I politely thanked Xavier for calling and giving me the opportunity, but I knew I was called to VO. My heart should have been light, but it was heavy. I was sad and lonely and had just said 'no thank you' to my dream job. *God, you had better help me through this. You sent me here. You showed me clearly that I'm called to VO to run the women's home.*

A few weeks later, a lady called Marcia came to the shop to buy some cards. She was friendly and seemed interested in me and visiting the church. We struck up a good friendship and started to pray together. She lived close by, so we were able to spend time together. Brian and I were spending a bit of time together as well, going into London in the evenings and going out for tea together. I found him funny and interesting. He had a great prayer life and knew the Word well. He was in the ministry, doing the sound, and was in a small group. Coming from being a six-stone heroin addict with nothing to live for, he was a real trophy of God's grace. I was starting to have feelings for him. I felt awful; he was so young! He was only 23 and I was 37. I had been married twice before and nearly married as a Christian as well. This wasn't good. What would people think?

It was time to pray and ask God for direction. Brian was lovely but he was far too young and inexperienced for me. He was not long out of the home. We continued to hang out together. Summer came, things were getting better, and I was beginning to feel more settled in the church, starting to connect with people, enjoying my job at Betty's and loving being a part of the healing rooms. The healing rooms training had been incredible. Betty and Tom were a wealth of experience and faith. It was creeping in that I was spending too much time with Brian and really enjoying that time. My feelings had grown and were becoming hard to contain. I knew I needed to say something to him, but the fear of him laughing at me or telling everyone that this old woman had feelings for him was killing me!

I decided that it had to be done. It was getting to the end of July and we had been out and were having our dinner at the house we shared with Christians from other churches. We had finished eating and Brian was clearing the table. I said to him to sit down for a minute and told him very quickly and clearly that we couldn't go out and about any more, as my feelings had changed and I was not his friend any more, but was in love with him. His face was a picture; he went chalk-white and said nothing. He slowly rose from the table and silently left the room! My mind was racing around like wasps buzzing in my head. *What have I just done? Really? What a car crash that was. Shall I knock on his room and apologise? Shall I say, "Oh sorry, only kidding"?* No I couldn't do that, because I wasn't kidding. Instead, I slowly walked up the stairs to my room and sank to the floor, knowing I had just made the biggest fool of myself ever. What were people going to say about me?

I realised really quickly I still had to work with him. *Oh no! How embarrassing is that going to be? Maybe I can call in sick?* I decided to pop out to the shops for a couple of Bacardi Breezers. Who remembers them? The pineapple ones were my favourites. Two was always enough. I was super-proud of the fact I could occasionally have a couple of these and no more. I wasn't sinking into addiction or anything; I had full control over having just one or even two. Saying that, there are some who, after addiction, are not able to do this, and it would cause them to sink back into that black hole of destruction. So, be careful: this was OK for me, but may not be OK for you.

Another guy from the church was also living in the house. He was a right character; my officially adopted brother. Lots of people thought we were actually brother and sister and, to our minds, we were. He was hilarious and deadly at the same time, would help anyone with a need, and was always ready to lift up and support the underdog. Barry was certainly a one-off. We got on very well and had great laughs together. He told me to just forget about him and move on. I knew I was going to have to, as the reaction I got, or lack of it, told me all I needed to know.

I was dreading the next morning. I had hardly slept a wink. We usually met at the bottom of the stairs to walk to work together, but I was sure he would have gone on without me. What was work going to be like? To my utter surprise, Brian was waiting at the bottom of the stairs for me! Not one word was uttered about what had been said the day before. We just moved on without addressing it. I was thinking to myself, *well, if he's not bothered about it, neither am I. Why be awkward about it?* It was done and dusted as far as I was concerned, but in my heart I knew God had placed him in my heart to be my husband.

It was so strange and unreal. Life moved on. I continued to pray about it and to find my feet in the church. Marcia was fast becoming a real good friend. She was funny and clever too. Marcia is the queen of cards;

always has and sends a card for every occasion. A true encourager.

Brian and I were still firm friends, but not going out for dinner or going to London on our own. I felt it wasn't healthy, knowing how I felt. Brian was asked out a couple of times by other people, as was I, but to say they didn't work out was not really cutting it. One of my suitors wanted to take me away on a boat, and another was standing outside the shop waiting on me when Brian told me he was married. That was a no-go, for sure.

Time marched on. It was getting towards the end of September and I was involved in some aspects of ministry at the church and getting to know people a bit better. It was a Sunday like any other Sunday, and I was getting ready for church. Barry had given me a couple of his work shirts to iron, which I did regularly for him. I hung them on the back of the kitchen door and off I went to church.

After service, somehow we all ended up arriving home at the same time. Brian went in first and went straight over to the shirts hanging neatly ironed on the door and threw them on the ground, stood on them, pointed to me and said, "You are never going to iron another man's shirts again!"

Barry was fuming and started a row with him. I went straight up the stairs after shouting at him, "Who do you think you are talking to?" I shut the door of my room and tried to make sense of what had just happened. I just couldn't. It didn't make sense. Why would Brian be carrying on like that, out of the blue?

I was in my room pottering about, praying a bit, overthinking a bit, worrying a bit. What was going on?

I didn't see Brian or Barry for the rest of the day, but their row was epic. Evening had set in and I was reading in my room when the door knocked. I wondered for a moment who it was? Brian or Barry? Did I even want to answer it? I opened the door to find a red-in-the-face Brian standing there. He has lovely red hair, so he was almost glowing at the top of the stairs with the big red face and the hair. He looked at me right in the eyes and said he was just letting me know that we would be getting married! What? What on earth was he talking about? I just shut the door in his face after saying, "If that's the case, you will ask me properly."

I didn't get one wink of sleep that night. What was happening? I knew he was going to be my husband, but it wasn't exactly the love story I had imagined.

As per usual, Brian was waiting at the bottom of the stairs for me to go to work the next morning. *Shall I mention the night before or not?* I decided not to. Lunchtime came at work and I was glad of the break; it had been a very busy morning and my head was fried thinking about how to talk to Brian about what he had blurted out the night before. I had just sat down with my avocado salad bowl when Betty shouted me to come in to the healing rooms. I certainly didn't mind having to pray for someone, but I did wish I had been able to eat first. As I walked into the room, there was Brian standing with Betty. He went straight down on one knee and produced a gorgeous ring in a little blue box and asked me properly to marry him. To say my gob was smacked is a little short of the mark. God, you are truly amazing, but please don't do anything that way again!

Betty was delighted. She told me she had known straight away when I came to work at the shop that Brian and I would be married. I was floating on cloud nine and giving thanks all over the place. The battle was just beginning, little did I know.

Brian called pastor Mitchell to let him know we were engaged. He was pretty surprised; as far as most people knew, we had never been a couple. I didn't really think about the reaction to our announcement. I really wish I had. Sunday arrived and it was announced that we had got engaged. The atmosphere was a bit weird, which wasn't surprising, as we weren't known as a couple. Even Barry had been a bit surprised when we told him on the

Monday night. A few people came over to say congratulations, which was nice. I had one young woman signal me over to say she couldn't believe it, as she had always thought I was Brian's mum. I wasn't sure if she was being cheeky or not, but the comment stung and made me feel angry. My initial reaction was to slap her face, but I didn't; I just walked away feeling the burn of feeling talked about in a negative way. I started wondering if most people were thinking the same? There was a really big age gap. It's more the norm that older men marry younger women, and not so common the other way round. My only choice was to believe that God knew what He was doing.

I called Mum to tell her, wondering what she would make of it all and the age gap. She was great, and reminded me her husband was a good bit younger than her. I called Maggie Mum to tell her as well. She was delighted for us. She had been quite unwell for a while, so I thought good news might cheer her up a bit.

The reaction to our news in general at church was a mixture of disbelief, hostility and some good wishes. We had one person telling us there was no way God had put us together. I sensed a lot of jealousy going on and had to put all the negativity to the back of my mind. Brian was experiencing some negative responses as well. It threw us very close to each other; we only had each other to talk to really about what we were experiencing.

Inevitably, our closeness became sexual. We had more than one moment of, let's just call it unbridled passion, regretting it almost immediately but, once those floodgates were opened, it was hard to stem the flow. We arranged our wedding for the 28th of January in Falkirk, our hometown, to have all our family there with us. Brian moved out of the house we shared to stop the flow of sex. As Christians, our intention was to stay away from that area until we had been married, but it wasn't something we had been able to do. It was a real feeling of failure in that area. Does God forgive that kind of awful sin? Of course, He does. We were sorry; we knew God had called us to be together. Telling other people was hard: that sense of judgement, of feeling less of a Christian than other people who did save themselves for marriage. Back then, it was so difficult to talk about without feeling mucky. I'm in a position now where, after 18 years of marriage to my amazing Brian, I'm happy to share that we were, are, less than perfect. Honesty is the best policy.

We had from the beginning of October to the end of January to arrange our wedding in Scotland. My mentor and closest friend, Nora, was a dressmaker. I drew a picture and described what I wanted and she made me the most incredible, one-off wedding dress. It was gold, in a Celtic style with a little, fitted, bolero-style jacket. Barry was the best man, and they were in Pride of Scotland kilts. Moira took on the food, providing an amazing buffet on a tight budget. Evelyn took on the decoration and Leigh Anne sang our favourite song as we left the church married. I know the *Master of the Wind*, which had been sung by her on the night that Brian had made the decision to ask Jesus into his heart and begin his journey of faith.

Our prayer life had been very much around God providing for our wedding, and also that all we wanted was some fruit from our covenant to Him for each other. On the day before the big day, I still had no shoes. My budget had been halved as Brian's brother John needed shoes. I was in despair looking for the right shoes for the big day. The dress was so spectacular that I didn't want to ruin it with cheap pumps. January isn't the best time to look for shoes for a wedding! I found a little dance shop in a back street that Nora put me on to and, in there, I found a pair of white wedding shoes with the exact same brocaded look as my dress front. They were just lying there in a little stack of shoes, looking very expensive. I picked them up and went to ask about them. I told her what they were for and how they matched the dress. There was no box for them, so she knocked a tenner off, giving me a fiver left from my shoe budget to go and quietly sit in a cafe and thank God for them.

It was Bible study night at The Peoples Church that night, and our rehearsal for the big day the next day. Pastor Paul and his wife, Vicky, were up to be a part of our big day, as we wanted him to be a part of the ceremony somehow. He had been instrumental in Brian coming to Victory Outreach, as he had led the team to Falkirk in 2001. The night went well. There were lots of people there and one young man had come in that night to see about getting help for his addiction. Pastor McKim asked Barry and pastor Paul and Vicky to give a word of testimony that night, and that was the catalyst for Kevin Keenan heading off to the Victory Outreach men's home. When we heard about it, we were delighted, and made a vow to pray him through the home.

Our wedding was amazing. We were very happy to see our families all there with us and had asked specifically that the gospel be preached so that all of our families heard the call to come to Jesus. We had no money for a honeymoon and, even if we had, we didn't have enough time off work to go on one. We wanted to be a part of The Peoples Church anniversary celebrations and give our testimonies at the weekend. Maggie Mum (natural mum) was in hospital in Edinburgh receiving radiotherapy for a tumour she had. My friend Denise (she's going to be upset that I've said her name) paid for a night in a fabulous hotel next to the hospital Maggie was in. Brian had never met her. She wasn't in her bed when we arrived, so Brian went down to the cafe to get some snacks. I was waiting for him to come out of the lift and, when the lift doors opened, there was Maggie and Brian in the lift totally unaware they had found each other. It was a strange visit, mixing our good news with Maggie's not-so-good news about her treatment and tumour.

Off we went to start our married life in London. We were both still working at Betty's; Brian was now the manager of the shop and I was doing the wages and administrative jobs, as well as shifts in the shop. We loved it. Our wages were great, and we had received more than £3,000 in gifts from our wedding guests. We were going to save up for a proper honeymoon somewhere hot and fabulous. We have never gone anywhere hot and fabulous to just relax and enjoy.

A marriage retreat was scheduled for the beginning of March with the church in Manchester where Paul and Vicky were leading the church. They had been sent up in the October to take over from another couple who were coming back to London. We decided it was something we should invest in. We asked Betty and Tom for a couple of days off to attend it, and the reply was that only one of us could go. It seemed a bit pointless one of us going.

Mid-March brought an invitation to have dinner with pastor Mitchell and Sis Nellie. We were a bit nervous as we had got engaged with them not knowing we were a couple. We married very quickly as we felt better to marry than to keep having sex.

The dinner went well. They were great company, the food was amazing, and it was good to get to know them a little better. For me, anyway. Towards the end of the evening, the conversation turned towards pastor Paul and Vicky in Manchester. They were looking for a couple to join them in Manchester to help rebuild the church. We were a bit taken aback. We were just married, had fantastic jobs we loved. What were the prospects of work in Manchester? Where would we live? The questions were massive.

We decided to think about it and pray about it. We knew we would enjoy working and ministering with pastor Paul and Vicky, because we had good relationships with them. We decided to go to Manchester, but only for a year to help. It was a huge decision to leave the security of our very well-paid jobs and our secure and happy accommodation to head off into the complete unknown. Manchester was looming. We were in touch with pastor Paul and Vicky, and they had organised for us to stay in someone's house they were not living in at that time. Sounded good.

We arrived in Manchester on the 6th of April, 2004, married just over two months, and six months after pastor Paul and Vicky had arrived. We settled in OK. We had to move quite quickly to another house, in Abbey Hey. It was in a real Coronation Street-looking area: deprived and rough. We were looking for work and had no success. Our savings were running out fast paying rent, buying bus passes to get everywhere, food and giving. We applied for all sorts of jobs, but nothing was successful. We had no bed in the new house; we were sleeping on the floor. My sister bought us a mattress and had it delivered. What a blessing that was. The rent was due, and we had no money, no benefits, nothing. Brian had managed to get a job in McDonald's in Salford, but from Gorton where we lived, it was a huge distance away. We had no food and would eat the free meal Brian got at the end of his shift.

It was getting beyond a joke. Where was God in this lack? Where was God in the state we were in? I walked out to meet Brian from work one day and, on the walk back, I found five pence. I thought, *if I find another 10p we can get a can of beans.* Unbelievably, we found a five pound note not far from home. We were delighted. It was a blazing hot day, and we went into a shop and bought two Magnum ice lollies. They were amazing, tasted so nice. We went to the Co-op and carefully spent the rest of the fiver, not knowing where our next meal was coming from; Brian didn't get any wages for another eight days.

We strolled home, praying the rain would stay off for the next eight days for Brian walking between Salford and Gorton. I was so glad to see our little house. It was too hot, and we had been walking for hours. There was post lying, and I made tea and sat down to open the letters. Mum had sent us a letter. I was hoping there was nothing wrong. In the letter there was a cheque for £500 and an explanation saying that when they had sold their house there had been some money over and they had decided to give us all something. I was jumping round the room thanking God for taking care of us yet again. It had been so difficult, but the tide was turning. Brian had a job, and I had an interview for a cafe in town.

Big John, as we all fondly called him, came to live with us as his re-entry time after leaving the Victory Outreach men's home. He was easy to live with and had his sights set on work. He had a strong Christian family behind him; his mum was amazing. I felt a bit sorry for him coming to live with us newlyweds struggling to acclimatise to each other and all the new surroundings etc. He made it through seven months of living with us and went on to share a flat with another guy we fondly called little John.

Meanwhile, back in our house, we had news that we had to move out real quick as the landlord was selling. Where would we go? We started to look for rented accommodation, but everything was out of our reach. We were not ready to move, with no deposits or rent up front. Big John's mum, Christine, offered us a room in her house until we had saved enough to move. She lived very far out of the city in Offerton. It was a great place to live, but a challenge to get to work and church all the time. We were so grateful to have been given this opportunity to save, and save we did. We found a great place in Heaton Mersey to live. It was the beginning of 2006. In 18 months, we had moved four times.

Another move was coming right up, little did we know. We had become part of the church and had seen so much growth, not only in numbers but in faith and strength. Our desire to go back to London was gone; we were fully immersed in seeing and working hard to see the church grow.

We were both in employment. I had a job in a care home for adults with learning difficulties, and did weekend shifts and sleepovers. I was also fully committed to all the administrative jobs and accounts for the church. This meant that, for nearly four years, I worked from 6 p.m. to 9 a.m. in the care home in Didsbury, then made my way across the city to Ordsall to work in the church office, which was in the men's home. Unless you're from Manchester, you're not going to know how big a journey this was but, trust me, it was far. I would finish up there and travel back to Didsbury to start my shift at 6 p.m. most days. The church was not financially well, so my payment was £50 a week for the church, and there were a couple of times we didn't have it to give me in the early days. Pastor Paul and Vicky were desperately trying to build from a not-very-secure foundation. But, with the work, prayer and time that was poured in over those early years and with some very faithful tithers, the church became fluid financially and was doing well.

Receipts were the bane of my life: credit card receipts, purchase receipts, event receipts. I prepared the accounts to be sent off to be signed off. I didn't have any fancy programs or graphs or anything like that; I had just been taught very simply to reconcile the outgoings with the receipts page by page alongside the bank statement pages. I filled in the QuickBooks program with areas we had spent the money in, which was pretty simple if it was kept up to date, which it was. I loved it. I felt that I was doing so much to help see people give their lives to the Lord. I was doing it in my own way as, no, I'm not the best at shouting down a microphone about how Jesus changed my life. No, I'm not very good at evangelising on the streets. But I was very good at keeping things nice and tidy behind the scenes, to help those that were good at the other stuff. It was certainly a labour of love, hand could be pretty tense at times. I prayed more in that season than most seasons in my life, I can tell you. It never ceased to amaze me how God saw every bill paid and more over.

The summer season was in full flow. We were so happy in our gorgeous little flat in a big Edwardian manse that had been split up into said flats. We had great people come and stay with us, including Betty and her cousin all the way from the US of A. Betty remains a close friend to this day. We had Zak stay for a little while after he came out of hospital after a miraculous recovery from being on life support.

Sunday, June the 25th, became a huge turning point. We went to church as normal. It was the home director's birthday, and we had bought him something really special and were looking forward to him opening his gift. He never came to church, as he had left the ministry and was off doing his own thing. It was a huge blow for the pastor, as it's not just anyone who can take on the home.

We were devastated. We went home after church in utter disbelief. How were we going to keep the home stable and steady for the guys? Pastor Paul arrived at our house just before teatime, and he had the weight of the world on his shoulders. We knew what he was going to ask before he even got out of the car. Were we ready?

That night, we went over to the home. I slept on the bed as there was only a single bed in the room, and Brian slept on the floor. Brian was now running the home. The weight of it was intense: there were six guys in the home and all were needing some stability. We did our best, and inevitably some left, but some stayed. New men came in and out over the next seven months. It was exhausting. Brian had given up his job, but I was still working in

Didsbury and doing all the admin and accounts. Now I was also doing the home's accounts and admin.

The building was falling apart, and it was fast becoming apparent that we couldn't be in there much longer. There was not one room where the door shut properly, so we had no privacy, and as a female in the men's home, that was not ideal. I struggled greatly with old feelings of being attacked, and my fear of something bad happening in there was immense, considering what I had gone through. We wanted to be a support, and helpful in taking on the role when there was no one really to do it at that time. God knows what we did, and we have been rewarded over the years for our sacrifice.

There was one tiny shower that we all used. I got baths etc. at my work, which was a godsend. The building was in a really deprived area and was attacked often. We had stones thrown through the windows and had fireworks poked into the windows and set off. They even set the roof on fire once. I had had enough. I had been attacked twice; once by a guy who was simply desperate for drugs and, another time, the guy just didn't like me. Brian was struggling under the weight of it too. A new house had been bought but would take time to get ready, and the home had to close down as it was being knocked down to make way for a regeneration project in Ordsall. Brian was asked to continue as the director but made the decision – not lightly, by the way – to say no, he was not able to take on the role again. It had been such a hard season, and we were both exhausted.

The news didn't go down very well, as it left the home with no director again but, we reasoned, at least there was time to pray until the new house was ready to need a director.

Brian was very kindly re-employed by Wesley Owen, and I continued in my two jobs. My new office was still in the men's home, but in Salford, which was slightly easier to get to but still a real distance from work.

Where was God in all this? A question I asked myself often; surely things were meant to be great when you were a Christian? Didn't God and the angels sweep all our troubles away? Wasn't life supposed to be so much easier as a Christian? No. Unfortunately, life still goes from high to low, as it does for all other people of all faiths. It's how we manage the highs and lows, how we keep ourselves grounded in prayer and studying the Word. I'm great at prayer and Brian is great at studying the Word. We complement each other well.

We moved twice; once into our friend's attic until we got a house in Gorton. It was a nice, two-bedroom little terrace house in Argyll Street which was being championed as a Caleb project, where a house is bought and rented to Christians to bring Christ into the street. We settled into our new abode and life went on.

As I'm sure all wives will say about their husbands, my husband is attractive inside and outside. He has a great physique and gorgeous red hair, blue twinkly eyes and a knock 'em out smile. He is fairly naïve as well, which is endearing, but he seemed to attract all the wrong kind of attention. One Sunday morning, I was busying myself getting the Kids' Gang room ready at the Palace Hotel, where we had our Sunday services. A young lady from the church came and asked to speak to me. I thought she wanted advice or prayer or something, but she wanted to tell me she was in love with my husband. *In love with my husband?* My brain was screaming. *Has he been having an affair? Is this girl for real? What's going on?*

The old me started to roar inside. *Give her a slap. Throw her out on the road.* Imagine coming to seek me out to tell me this. The new me took a breath, looked away from her and prayed, *help me Lord not to knock this girl clean out on the floor here.* She began to explain that she was in love with him but he was completely unaware of it. She had even been stalking him for weeks at Wesley Owen. I began to see that most of this was in her head. Brian hadn't encouraged her. She began to cry and say she was sorry. I wrapped her up in my arms and prayed for her. Over the years, I've read love letters written to my husband and had phone calls from people telling me they are in love with my husband. So much was designed to smash our marriage on the rocks. Being a twice-divorced woman whose husbands have gone off with other women, what better way to try to get into this marriage with lies to try to end it too. No sir, I'm not falling for that one. My marriage is for keeps. I adore my husband and I'm 1,000 per cent sure he loves and adores me too. God brought us together to stay together.

We rolled into 2008 with another move looming. The church had rented a seven-bedroom house in the heart of Moss Side. We were asked to move in and run it as a discipleship house for some of the young women in the church. We had a great time there and thoroughly enjoyed it. The women were great, we had lots of fun and built great relationships.

In that year, we went off in the summer as usual to help Wesley Owen build and work in their shop at the Keswick convention. Brian wanted to climb the ladder through promotion within the company. He had been praying about it. He came home after a long walk and said he knew he was going to go into management. He said if he went on the website and saw a position, he would apply. He did, and applied for a job in Croydon. They were delighted to have him train for a senior position. Brian fully believed this was all from God, even though it meant moving away from all that we had loved in Manchester. Not everyone believed this move was from God, and we endured a very difficult time where, again, God stepped in and made a way for us when we found ourselves very suddenly homeless. We arrived in London battered and hurting inside, but with a strong resolve to do our best in this new venture God had led us into.

It wasn't long until things came tumbling down around us. Brian was offered another opportunity somewhere else and took it. This was the beginning of the end. We were now living in an adapted shed; it was OK, but not ideal. In prayer one morning, I heard God say it was time to go home. It's always been my dream to go back to Scotland to live. This has still to come to pass fully. My understanding of home at that point was Scotland. So, off we went and moved all the way back up to Falkirk, where we had both come from. Again, this was not all we had hoped for. We couldn't find work, and were not allowed benefits. I have to give thanks to my friend, who paid our rent for four months. I'm eternally grateful. The flat was tiny. To get in the bathroom to go to the toilet you had to walk all the way to the sink and turn round to shut the door to allow you enough room to sit on the toilet. I've never seen such a small bathroom since, and I don't wish to see one like that ever again.

It didn't take long for the strain to take its toll on our marriage. We were living on little amounts of money from casual cleaning jobs, and the generosity of others.

We kept falling out. I kept blaming Brian for the mess we were in; he was the one who took the other opportunity instead of sticking to God's plan. I was disappointed, frustrated, fed up and so angry at him and life in general. It came to boiling point one evening when I lost my temper and chucked him out and told him not to come back, because it was over, and I had had enough. Inside, I knew everything was all wrong: we were not where we were supposed to be, nothing was going right, and we couldn't seem to get up. In utter desperation I phoned Vicky, our pastor's wife from VO Manchester. It had been a difficult decision to leave, and a difficult season for them that we had moved in. After tears and explanations as to where we were, she told us to go back to Manchester. God made a way for us to go back and we settled in well. I realised that when God said to go home, He meant to Manchester, not Scotland.

Life rolled on with its ups and downs. We moved into our own place and got work, and things began to repair in our marriage. I'm thankful to everyone who helped us through that season.

Let's move on through the years to January 2013. Do you remember me saying I wanted to run a women's home? I always believed I was called to work with and minister to women. I finally got the call to ask if I would take over the women's home in Manchester. Absolutely; of course I will. How soon do you want me? I had been waiting since 2003 for this to come to pass. It had been 10 years of waiting, saying no to other, similar opportunities. It was my time to shine and do what God had called me to do. After 10 years of growing in God, I was not ready at any point in the 10 years to run a women's home. Now was the chosen time for this part of the calling that God had placed on my life.

There were four women in the home when I was told I would be taking over and, by the time me and Brian moved in, they had all left. *Great start. What an anointing you have there Fiona,* I said to myself. One of the girls came back after a couple of weeks and we saw her through to graduation. The homes are amazing little incubators for people to come and get their lives sorted out through good discipline and learning better habits and, most importantly, coming to know that there is a God and He does love you, no matter what you have done in your life, then accepting His son the Lord Jesus Christ as your saviour.

The women came in over the next four years broken, battered, addicted and completely messed up. Eleven of them graduated the programme, and many didn't graduate but went on to live changed lives. Many went back out into the madness. We had many characters in through those doors, with each one prayed for and led to the Lord. Over the years we broke up fights, saved lives, cried with families. We saw God move in wonderful ways in women's lives.

Brian was amazing with the women. His wisdom saved the day many a time. When I had come to the end of myself, Brian would cut in and do something amazing to change the whole atmosphere of the home. Many women from the church brought their wisdom to the women, and many taught them to cook, let them cry on their shoulders and taught them how to war in the heavenlies. It was the best four years of my life. I pay homage to the women that made it through the rigours of the home: Theresa John; Kiera McCormack; Jordanna Carrol; Laura Nicolson; Emma Anthony; Liz McCorgary; Aisling Bradley; Nicola Downie; Laura Mitchell, Emma Slevin. and Maria Breen. We also had Tina Voordouw, who graduated after spending many months working with us and living in the home. God had shown me there would be many graduates, that fruit would be evident as I ploughed the fields. I had been for a coffee with my pastor's wife, Vicky, as I took on the home, and she had been given a word from one of her prayer team to say that there would be at least ten graduates in my season as director. And, sure enough, there were ten graduates, most of whom are living drug-free lives to this day.

September 2016 – it was time to leave the home. My heart was breaking. I loved every moment of being in the home, and would have stayed in it for the rest of my life if I could. I had loved every single woman that had walked through the doors, and poured my all into each life that wanted it. I had agonised and cried over the many that left. I had blamed myself for not doing enough, beaten myself up over lives lost back into addiction and realised that it was the choices people made. No, I'm most certainly not perfect, and neither are you. What I do know is the next chapter of my life was about to burst into action. God had brought His promise of a child to me and I was about to embark on parenthood at 50 years of age, as Brian was about to battle testicular cancer.

Look out for book number two, called *This is Me – I'm Adopted*. This book will focus on the pain of disconnection, rejection and abandonment. It will also incorporate my 33 years of infertility and loss of three children. It will finish with God bringing our beautiful promise to pass of a child, at 50 years of age.

THIS IS ME
FIONA MYLES

This is me Fiona Myles born in the mid-sixties. I am'
married to the amazing Brian a gorgeous redhead. We
have one daughter called Georgie who is five and one son
Connor who is 21.

Manchester has been our home for the past 18 years a
fabulous metropolis full of energy and history.

I started writing stories from a fairly young age. My Mum bought me a typewriter when I was around eight or nine years old. I battered away at that little typewriter, day in and day out, for a while. Life moved on and so sadly did the typewriter.

Fast forward 45 years and the birth of the laptop which becomes my new typewriter. My passion for writing was reignited during the awful time of the national lockdown in 2020.

This is Me - No Darkness too Deep is a testimonial book of my roller coaster journey through life.

You can find out more about me and my books by visiting my website.

www.fionamylesauthor.com

connect with me on facebook and Instagram
Fiona Myles Author

This is Me
No Darkness too Deep

An Autobiography
By
Fiona Myles

www.marciampublishing.com

Printed in Great Britain
by Amazon